Joanna Ramsey's poetry and short fiction have
appeared in *Chapman, New Writing Scotland* and
other magazines and anthologies. Two pamphlet
collections of poems have been published by the
Galdragon Press, Glasgow: *In Memory of George
Mackay Brown* (1998) and *Walking on Hoy*
(2002). She lives in Orkney and also works as a
copy-editor for academic publishers.

The
SEED BENEATH
The
SNOW

Remembering George Mackay Brown

JOANNA RAMSEY

SANDSTONE PRESS
HIGHLAND | SCOTLAND

First published in Great Britain
and the United States of America
Sandstone Press Ltd
Dochcarty Road
Dingwall
Ross-shire
IV15 9UG
Scotland.

www.sandstonepress.com

© Joanna Ramsey 2015
Editor: Moira Forsyth

The publisher acknowledges subsidy from
Creative Scotland towards publication of this volume.

ISBN: 978-1-910124-51-2
ISBNe: 978-1-910124-52-9

Front cover: From the Gunnie Moberg Archive at Orkney Library & Archive
Frontispiece: Image by Angela Catlin, reproduced by permission

Cover design by Raspberryhmac Creative Type, Edinburgh
Typeset by Iolaire Typesetting, Newtonmore
Printed and bound by Totem, Poland

For Emma, with my love

CONTENTS

ACKNOWLEDGEMENTS

I should like to express my warm thanks to all those who encouraged me to write this book, especially Moira Burgess and Brian Murray, and to those friends who read a late draft of the manuscript and made many valuable suggestions: Moira Burgess, Tim Morrison, Brian Murray, Liza Murray, Jeanne Bouza Rose and Nigel Wheale. Moira Burgess also supplied some good anecdotes and articles, and shared some of George's letters to her, and Brian and Liza Murray have been wonderfully helpful in sourcing information. Cary Welling advised on earlier drafts of two chapters; Carl MacDougall allowed me to draw upon his recollections of the first time he visited Stromness; and Keith Allardyce contributed an anecdote about George and Nora. Erlend Brown gave information about some of the paintings once owned by George, and also kindly let me look through George's own collection of photographs. Rebecca Marr was generous with her time in arranging for me to view images from Gunnie Moberg's photographic archive, and other staff at the Orkney Library & Archive also gave assistance. Fiona Cumming provided information about a folio of poems and prints to which George contributed. Jim Lawson's reminiscences and comments have been helpful and reassuring.

I am immensely grateful to Sandstone Press, for their rapid response to my submission and for all their support. Moira Forsyth has been a marvellous editor and given me invaluable advice.

My sincere thanks also go to Archie and Elizabeth Bevan and to the Estate of George Mackay Brown for giving me permission to quote from George's letters to me, and from his poems and journalism, and to reproduce an unpublished poem and several acrostics.

I was delighted by Angela Catlin's kindness in allowing me to use her evocative portrait of George, and I thank her for her generosity. I am much obliged to Fiona Shaw, who clarified details about her performances; and also to Kathleen Lucky, Television Curator at the BFI's National Film Archive, for tracking down the transmission dates of several programmes.

Finally, I want to express my gratitude to my wonderful daughter, Emma, for all her love and support, and for sharing in my happiness that this book is to be published.

I have tried to give an accurate account of events that happened many years ago, my recollections being substantiated by notes, diary entries and letters, but I trust that anyone whose version of past incidents differs from my own will understand the vagaries of memory.

INTRODUCTION

George Mackay Brown and I first met in the summer of 1988, when he was in his sixties and I was thirty-five. At that time I had not read any of his books and knew almost nothing about him, but I guessed that our backgrounds and experiences would have been very different. Yet within a few weeks we had become friends, and the friendship grew and continued – if precariously at times – for a period of eight years until the day of his death in 1996. Early in 1989 he wrote a poem for me, about the tentative pleasures of gradually becoming closer to another person:

How comes this, Joanna? Slowly
Through a late summer, an autumn,
    A half winter, we have
    Come to know each other

(Not that, in this time of 'vanitas'
Anyone can *really* know another,
    But sometimes, among the shadows and rocks
    One rock utters brightness,

Someone has brought a jar, a fragrance lingers),
So now, when you leave the islands
    For London, a five-day absence, I think
    'This will be a drab weekend' . . .[1]

After George died, I began to realise that perhaps I hadn't known him as well as I thought I had. When I read the obituaries, I was sometimes scarcely able to recognise him. Many of my memories of him are threaded with his humour and his sense of fun, but the person portrayed there in newsprint seemed an altogether more sombre figure. That is not to say that George was always cheerful during his last decade – far from it. I know that he suffered deeply. In a letter written to me in 1991, from his hospital bed in Aberdeen, he spoke of being exhausted and 'darkly depressed'. But I am quite certain that in those later years he also experienced a keen enjoyment of life and many moments of quiet contentment. Delight was still to be found in the lines and colours of the Orkney landscape; in the company of friends and relations; in art, music and literature; and in the various processes of his own work. When I think of George, the image that comes most often into my mind is not the rather haggard, melancholy face that has sometimes accompanied articles or appeared on the dust jackets of books about him, but a much happier, smiling man sitting next to my young daughter, Emma Catherine Lawson, and making her laugh with his teasing and his songs.

George wrote a poem for Emma, 'A New Child: ECL – 11 June 1993', and included it in his collection *Following a Lark*.[2] One of the reasons for beginning this book was that I wanted to tell the story behind that poem and to set down my recollections of George while I could do so with reasonable confidence in my own memory, before forgetfulness blurred the outlines of the past. I had written about some of our meetings and outings in notebooks, diaries and drafts of poems, and mentioned them in letters to my parents, Frank and Beryl Richardson, which they returned to me after George's death, but other incidents were becoming harder to recollect clearly and I was beginning to confuse a few dates and details.

I thought at first that it might be possible to tell a story that focused solely on George, recounting our meetings and conversations but leaving the rest of my life out of the picture. After writing just a few pages, however, I saw how unsatisfactory it would be to do that; it became clear that the narrative of our friendship needed a fuller setting. The waxing and waning of affection, and the joys and hurts of our times together, could not be described in any meaningful way without a wider context to make sense of them. Thus, while sifting through my memories of George, I had to summon up the person I was at the time when I met him – a woman who had run away, in a manner of speaking, from her life in London; who was trying to carve out a niche for herself in a new place; who found great joy in being in Orkney but was sometimes sad and frequently self-absorbed. I was an unlikely companion for George, perhaps, but when I look again at that lovely poem he wrote, 'For Joanna', I dwell on the word 'brightness' and find some comfort in it – George saw more than the darkness in me.

The story has other characters too, who were very much a part of our lives at that time. They include George's relatives, his many friends and some of mine, and former lovers and partners. When I moved to Stromness, I found a sense of interconnectedness, of lives interwoven, that I had never experienced in cities or suburbia, and I wanted to explain how I came to be living in this remarkable community, and to set the scene for readers who have never visited the islands – to catch some of the sights, sounds and smells of Orkney: the light, the wind and the water; oystercatchers and curlews calling; peat smoke and seaweed. And although this book describes George's last years and his death, it also celebrates hope and resilience and renewal, and life's endlessly surprising possibilities.

I thought that the process of writing and remembering would in some way bring George a little closer again, or that I would understand him better with the benefit of hindsight, but it has not been quite like that. My sense of who and what he was seems even less certain now. All I can offer is a personal and partial view – a glimpse of an enigmatic but endearing man.

I

AN INCOMER

In the autumn of 1993, writing an appendix to his autobiography, *For the Islands I Sing*, George began: 'This autobiography was written in 1985. There is nothing much to add.'[1] In those two brief and perhaps rather cruel sentences, George seemed to dismiss most of the last decade of his life. He went on to acknowledge that 'new friends have appeared too, from time to time', but he did not refer to his continuing affection for his friend and former lover Nora Kennedy, or the joy he felt when he met Kenna Crawford, a young woman who inspired a number of his poems: 'A stranger came in / So beautiful / She seemed to be a woman from the sea'.[2] It has been said of Kenna that 'it pains and puzzles her that he never mentioned her in the 1993 appendix to his autobiography',[3] and I can imagine the similar anguish that Nora might have felt, although she never spoke of it. Surinder Punjya, an incomer to Orkney whose companionship was so important to George in the last years, appeared to be merely someone who did the shopping. A group of close relatives and friends had become, at this late reckoning, simply people who 'see to it that I don't starve'. They included one of George's nieces, Allison Dixon, her husband, Fraser, and their youngest child, Magnus, with whom George spent many pleasant Monday afternoons and Christmas holidays; Archie and Elizabeth Bevan, whose hospitality at Hopedale he always enjoyed so heartily; and Renée Simm, an elderly lady who moved to Orkney to be near George (she lived at Quildon Cottage on the Back Road in Stromness, within walking distance of his home), lavishing her attention and affection upon him.

There was not even the briefest account of the trips he took with the Orkney-based Swedish photographer Gunnie Moberg to Shetland in 1988, and London and Oxford in 1989 (although he wrote about them elsewhere), and there was very little about his many other friends or the hordes of visitors whom he received with apparently genuine delight at his small house in Mayburn Court. And of course I could hardly help noticing that I had no place there at all, nor was there any mention of my daughter Emma, born in the summer of 1993, for whom George wrote an exquisite celebratory poem, 'A New Child'.

Although there are lighter notes occasionally, the appendix to George's autobiography has a mournful tone and was surely written at a time when he was at a low ebb, succumbing to the feeling that nothing now could come to any good. He questioned his pleasure in listening to music – 'occasionally the uneasy thought, that there is something suspect about playing the same Beethoven or Mahler recording over and over' – and took a negative view of things that in my company he had often enjoyed and praised: 'The turning of great books into television drama is nearly always a failure.'[4] These comments suggest that, at the time of writing, the darkness had descended upon him again. But just as it had rapidly fallen, so it would eventually lift, like the Orkney storm clouds that gave George more anxiety as he grew older: 'there was a joy in storms, the hay-stack levellers and the ravelled roof-slates. Now I feel uneasy as the growl in the gale's throat deepens.'⁵ Among the tempests there were calm days and bright gleams, and I know that there were times when he felt contented – even happy – during those last years, because he told me more than once that he felt happy and I had no reason to doubt him at such moments. There was a sense of having come through, as his own writing sometimes conveys: 'To have got so far alone / Almost to the seventieth stone / Is a wonder'.⁶ Some lines from one of his later poems, 'Summer and Winter' (1987), reinforce this idea of resilience and suggest the possibility of renewal:

> We must all
> Endure dark times and onsets of winter.
> No person born but has
> Storms, barren branches, and darkness.
>
> We should know that always and everywhere
> The seed is under the snow,
> Waiting,
> And always it thrusts up, unfolding in the garden
> [. . .]
>
> Each one
> Has sat with curtains drawn against winter.
>
> Each one has thought then
> The bleakness and cold never-ending.
>
> Listen to the summer music!
> The sea is blue again, the grass is green.⁷

Maggie Fergusson, in her fine biography of George, confirms my belief that his last decade was by no means an entirely dismal period, suggesting that although he was naturally affected by the deaths of a number of his old friends, there was nevertheless 'quite another side to this gloomy picture. Reading through the hundreds of letters George wrote to his friends in the last ten years of his life, the note of decline and dénouement is easily balanced by one of renewed vigour and appetite for life.'[8] That continuing enthusiasm, in spite of physical weakness, was certainly evident, especially during the early years of our friendship.

Seeing George for the first time, I was struck by his apparent fragility: he was a thin, angular man in his late sixties, with an unruly mass of thick grey hair, a gaunt face and a jutting chin. Later, catching sight of him as he negotiated the street on a windy day, I thought he might be swept off his feet at any moment, and his progress was slow as he went up the flight of steps to his front door. In spite of this he seemed to have a tenacious hold on life, and it became easy to convince myself – because I wanted so much to believe it – that he might have many more years ahead of him. Yet there were also evenings spent sitting beside his hearth when I would catch sight of his face, cast into shadow by the angle of the lamp, and be suddenly and painfully aware of his vulnerability, realising that everything could change in an instant, the whole lovely house of cards collapsing and bringing to an end these companionable times that I had come to value so greatly. 'It could end in a moment', I wrote in the draft of an unfinished poem, with a sense of dread at the prospect of losing him. Even after knowing him for a short time, life without him had become hard to imagine.

George and I met soon after I moved to Orkney. I was in

my mid-thirties then, divorced, childless and lacking a sense of direction. Born in London in the 1950s, I had been happy living there; at one time it seemed like the centre of the universe to me. But during the 1980s it changed perceptibly and became a noisier, more aggressive and less pleasant place to live. After I was mugged at the corner of my own street, I knew that I should do more than dream about moving away, and I began applying for jobs all over the country – anything that would make use of my background in libraries and archives. In the summer of 1987, I was having lunch one day with David Simpson, then the director of ASH (Action on Smoking and Health), whom I had met some years earlier when I worked for the Health Education Council. I was having a difficult time in a new job, and he said that he was setting off soon for a holiday in Orkney, a place he often visited, and asked if I would like to go too. Thus it was that I first crossed the Pentland Firth on a bright, windy August evening and saw Stromness sheltering under the hill known as Brinkie's Brae. For those who have never travelled to these islands, there is perhaps no better introduction than George's book *An Orkney Tapestry*, in which he reveals their powerful beauty. He writes of 'dawn mingling its fires with sunset' in June and July, and 'magnificent' January nights: 'star-hung skies, the slow heavy swirling silk of the aurora borealis, the moon in a hundred waters'.[9] As I soon discovered, the inhabitants of Orkney spend a lot of time talking about the weather – and with good reason, because its capriciousness tends to dominate their lives:

Nothing is more lovely than the islands in a shifting dapple of sun and rain . . . In the course of a single day you can

see, in that immensity of sky, the dance of sun, cloud, sea-
mist, thunder, rain: the endless ballet of the weather . . . In
later summer afternoons the wind goes through the corn
in deep, resonant surges, but the evenings are marvellously
tranquil, except for a broken thunder all along the west coast
of Orkney . . . the Atlantic, glutting itself among the caves
and rock stacks.[10]

I found myself completely captivated. David introduced me to
the architect Bashir Hasham and the three of us went to Rousay
for the weekend to stay with friends of Bashir's. At night I
heard seals calling in the darkness and I remember thinking
that I wanted to stay there forever. Reading the local paper, *The
Orcadian*, I saw a vacancy for the post of librarian at Kirkwall
Grammar School and applied for it on impulse, but I missed
the closing date and reluctantly had to accept that this just
wasn't meant to be. But the following spring, when I was having
supper at David's flat one evening, I picked up his subscription
copy of *The Orcadian* and saw that a qualified librarian was
needed at Stromness Academy. I applied the next day and my
parents were stoically supportive, although some of my friends
and colleagues seemed slightly horrified that I should seek such
a drastic change of lifestyle. David, however, thought it was an
entirely sensible idea, and urged me to contact his friends in
Orkney to tell them of my plans.

The first step towards this new life was an interview. 'On the
brink', I wrote in a notebook, 'I fly to Kirkwall on Monday &
back on Tuesday: if it doesn't change my life, at least I'll see
Orkney again.' It was a joyful moment when David Tinch, the
County Librarian at that time, rang to tell me that the job was

mine if I wanted it – and there was never really any doubt about that. I had a few weeks in which to pack up my belongings, rent out my flat and make arrangements to lodge my cat with my sister Jen Hicks, then on Friday 10 June 1988 I flew from Heathrow to Aberdeen and on to Kirkwall. As the plane made its descent, a surge of emotions – happiness, gratitude and fear – overwhelmed me and I found myself in tears. I had wanted life to change, and now it had changed beyond anything I could have expected; I felt as if I was arriving in another world. David's friend Elaine Gordon was at the airport to meet me and drive me to my lodgings, and as I got out of the car she handed me a bag of groceries to tide me over.

I had arranged to rent a house at Faravel in Stromness, but it was still being redecorated and I would stay for a few weeks in a flat at the north end of the town. On that first night I was too unsettled to sleep, and the fact that it never seemed to get dark was somehow unnerving. I was up early and went to Kirkwall on the bus to buy a bicycle, realising that I urgently needed transport of my own. In London I had travelled on the underground, or walked, and my inability to drive had hardly mattered, but I could see that here it would be a hindrance. Driving lessons must be a priority, but in the meantime a bike would have to do, although I hadn't ridden one for a decade or so. I found something suitable and set off back to Stromness feeling a little daunted by the fifteen-mile ride ahead of me, but I had gone barely a few hundred yards when a car stopped alongside and there was Elaine again, my good angel, saying that she could give me and the bike a lift as far as Finstown.

In the afternoon I walked the length of the winding street to the south end of Stromness, to have a look at my new home.

I went up the steps opposite Stromness Museum, passing George's house at 3 Mayburn Court without a second glance, since I did not know then that he lived at the south end. Nor did I know that he had just arrived back from a trip to Shetland with Gunnie Moberg and their friends Kulgin Duval and Colin Hamilton. George was not accustomed to travelling and he might well have been resting that afternoon, exhausted but euphoric after his holiday – 'loveliness beyond compare', he wrote in his 'Shetland Diary' on 31 May.[11]

My future home was the middle one in a terrace of three, with a lilac bush growing beside the door, and I realised that it would have a view of the sea and the Orphir hills. The streets of London seemed a million miles away, and in my notebook I wrote about an 'unimaginable change'. Next day I cycled to Yesnaby under a cloudless sky – noticing the colour of the Stenness Loch as I passed, 'unearthly in its brightness and intensity' – and sat watching the powerful waves surge at the base of the cliffs. I gazed at the view to the south, wondering whether I could really see 'the Old Man swirling in hazy cloud', trying to imagine what my life would be like in this wonderful place, not quite believing that it was real. I was so lost in my thoughts that I wasn't aware of the fierce heat of the sun, and was embarrassed to arrive for my first day at the Academy with a glowing red face. There seemed to be a great deal to learn there, as it was no small task to find my way around the apparently labyrinthine corridors and try to remember the names of the several hundred pupils who came into the library.

I was so preoccupied that the annual St Magnus Festival almost passed me by, but fortunately a colleague told me about it and I got last-minute tickets for a few events. One of these was the Johnsmas Foy, a celebration of George's work, held on 19 June in Stromness Town Hall, and there I heard for the first time some of the poems that would mean so much to me in years to come: 'Elegy' ('Now the lark's skein is thrown / About the burning sacrificial hill'); 'The Death of Peter Esson' ('Early on Monday last / There came a wave and stood above your mast'); and 'The Poet' ('His cold stare / Returned to its true task').[12]

In the meantime there were many new pleasures, one of which was 'seeing inside 18 Faravel for the first time & finding fresh cream paint on the walls, decent floorboards, huge walk-in cupboards – but of course, most of all, the view – eastward out to sea – every gradation of blue & green – hills & sea & sky'. Eventually the house was ready, and 'at the end of the day I went to the Town House, & the woman asked me to wait for Mr Tait a moment, & in came a large man carrying a lettuce & a bunch of radishes with earth on the roots. And I signed for the keys.' (There is a fine photograph of Oliver Tait in Keith Allardyce's book *Sea Haven*, which also contains images of some of the other people mentioned here, including George himself, Archie and Elizabeth Bevan, John Broom and Tam MacPhail, Erlend Brown, John Cumming, Ian MacInnes, Sir Peter Maxwell Davies, Gunnie Moberg, Sir Sidney Nolan and Sylvia Wishart.[13]) On the evening of 21 June I noted that 'the view of the harbour & Orphir [was] so lovely & yet somehow even *more* stunning was the *St Ola*, gliding past below my kitchen window'.

My furniture had been taken out of storage and safely delivered; I was at the Academy when it arrived, but one of the office staff told me that her grandmother had seen it being carried into my house. That was perhaps the moment at which I became properly aware of how many aspects of my new life would be under scrutiny; this would not always be easy for someone who had lived for years in the anonymity of a capital city. But in those first months everyone seemed friendly and keen to help: a neighbour came to the door and offered to cut my grass, and Bashir Hasham found a second-hand cooker for me. My family were eager to be helpful too, and Jen travelled up on the plane at the end of June, bringing Billie the cat. Her husband, Maurice, and younger son, Kevin, followed by car with my houseplants and a rosemary bush, as well as precious ornaments that I hadn't wanted to put in the removal van. They stayed for a few days to settle me in, and in return I showed them some of the beautiful places that I had discovered. It wasn't many weeks before other visitors from the south arrived, curious to see where I was, and life was full and interesting.

It wasn't all bliss, of course – there were darker moods, and moments when I wondered what on earth I'd done. But I was still sure that I had made the right decision. After a day's work, instead of squeezing into an underground train and walking home from the station along busy streets, I went to the beach at Warebeth (sometimes written as Warbeth) on fine evenings:

After two days of mist & rain, the miracle of light, & colour ... The corner of Hoy is almost not to be seen: the light blinds & dazzles ... Far out, the sea roars. Turning back, the light is kinder. One black sleek head as a seal approaches. The *Joma* throbs past, heading for Hoy ... Tam [MacPhail] & Gunnie [Moberg] pass, hand in hand. At the old Battery, firemen fight a fire: a black smudge of smoke mars the sky

above the hayfields. Returning, the house is quiet. White
sails break the shoreline of Stenness.

One morning at the end of July I arrived at the Academy to find
that two black bin-bags had been dumped beside the library
issue desk. Rummaging inside them, I found a quantity of
dusty treasures: books of all kinds, some of them first editions
and a number of them bearing the author's signature preceded
by the words 'To George'. Somewhat mystified, I asked around
among my colleagues and eventually the depute rector, Archie
Bevan, explained that the books were a gift to the school library,
as George Mackay Brown had been having a clear-out in order
to make room on his shelves for newer acquisitions. Over the
next few months I would spend many happy hours dusting,
sorting and cataloguing these books, gradually becoming more
familiar with some of the Scottish writers whose work I knew
only slightly. The first thing to do, however, was to thank
George for his generosity. I wrote to him and mentioned in
passing that we were almost neighbours. A few days later the
telephone rang at Faravel and I heard George's voice for the
first time, inviting me to have a cup of tea with him. In the
course of the conversation I mentioned that my friend David
Simpson was staying in Orkney for a few days and tentatively
asked if it would be all right to bring him along too, as I knew
he would like to meet George. There was no problem at all
about that – the more the merrier, apparently – and I realised
even then that perhaps George was not the reclusive man I had
been warned to expect.

A day or so later, George was greeting us kindly and ushering
us into his living room. I have no clear recollection of our

conversation that day, but what remains is a lasting impression of warmth and empathy. Robert Graves writes of 'friendship at first sight' (in his poem 'At First Sight') and perhaps that is what I experienced then: 'This also / Catches fiercely at the surprised heart'. I wrote to my parents on 4 August about having made two new friends during the previous week: one was Alison Blacklock, a school technician with whom I had many things in common (we even shared the same birthday), and the other was George. I mentioned my visit to Mayburn Court and added that one evening next week George was coming to have a cup of tea and meet Billie: 'He writes a column in the *Orcadian* each week and a friend's cat called Gypsy often features in his stories, so I am in hopes that one day Billie may be immortalised in print. GMB met David just after he had put in the cat door, and asked me all about Billie.'

As we left that day, George had urged me to call again, saying that I would be most welcome to go round at any time to see him, and in return I asked whether he would like to come to Faravel. I can still hear the playful tone of his reply – 'Oh yes, I would love to come round and meet the pussy-cat' – and my hope that Billie might feature in George's work was eventually fulfilled, as he wrote about her in *Letters to Gypsy*.[14] I didn't realise at the time, however, that he didn't think much of my address. 'What I don't particularly like is the giving of a fancy name like "Faravel" to a housing scheme', he had commented some years earlier in his column, which was called 'Under Brinkie's Brae'. 'It is too overtly flowery. It has no real meaning at all. And yet the name has caught on – these houses will be Faravel till they are empty shells.'[15]

After George's visit to Faravel, I was invited back to Mayburn

Court many times, and I gradually got to know him better. I had been given snippets of information about him by several of my new acquaintances in Orkney, but in a letter to my parents I confided that he was a much friendlier and less eccentric person than I had been led to believe. I wondered how well some of the people who were keen to tell me all about him really knew him; legends seemed to have grown around him. My letter described him as 'possibly quite lonely – in spite of having hordes of fans knocking on his front door in the summer' – but, whether he was lonely or not, it was endearing to find that in those first months he always seemed glad of my company. He rang me regularly, early in the evenings, asking me to visit him, and his name began to appear more frequently in my letters, diary and notebook.

In those years towards the end of his life, George tended to be a creature of habit and routine, and I tried to capture the spirit of our evenings together in a poem, describing his room full of books, pictures and flowers.[16] Some aspects of that room as it was in George's time elude my memory now, but others are still quite clear. As one entered from the small hallway there was a window to the left, facing north towards Brinkie's Brae, and another window opposite the door, facing east towards the sea and the Orphir hills. On the ledge of the sea-facing window was a collection of blue-green sea glass, brought piece by piece to Mayburn Court by Nora Kennedy. A large blue sofa facing the fireplace took up much of the space in the centre of the room, books and papers slipping down between its cushions, and behind it were low shelves crammed with books, with yet more volumes piled on top. To the right of the fireplace was George's rocking chair (currently in Stromness Museum), which had been given to him by a cousin when she left Orkney, and he thought that it was probably very old:

> Where countless thumbs have rested over the decades, the round wooden arm-bar is worn smooth on the right side . . . when one is agitated or happy or merely ticking over, it is the right thumb that caresses the woodwork, in sympathy with the motions of mind or mood . . . Sometimes, when I am feeling happy, I sing a wonderful blues song from the thirties: 'Old rocking chair's gonna get me . . .' The sentiment is melancholy but the music is full of joy.[17]

Along the wall beside the chair were shelves full of more books, music tapes, a row of whisky bottles and some engraved tumblers. At the far end of the room, below a south-facing window, were a dining table and chairs, and on the table there would be a dish of fruit and perhaps a plate and a cup; sometimes there were letters waiting for George's attention; once there were daffodils in a deep brown bowl. A glass-fronted cabinet stood between the table and the door into the kitchen. To the left of the south-facing window was one of the most striking features of the room: a wall-hanging, striped with horizontal layers of subtle colour and embroidered with words from the last stanza of a poem by Gerard Manley Hopkins, 'Inversnaid'. It was a lovely thing, finely made, and when I picture George sitting in his rocking chair I can still see it in my mind's eye, in the shadows behind him. Some years earlier, he wrote about how 'perhaps we are encroaching too deeply into the wilderness' and then added:

These thoughts were prompted by a beautiful gift that arrived before Christmas. It is a wall-hanging, a piece of exquisite embroidery, with words by my favourite poet Gerard Manley Hopkins stitched on it: 'What would the world be, once bereft / Of wet and of wildness? Let them be left, / O let them be left, wildness and wet; / Long live the weeds and the wilderness yet.' Hopkins loved cornfields and pasture; but he knew that in our dealings with Nature a balance must be struck and kept.[18]

George didn't say, however, who made the wall-hanging or gave it to him, and although it was included in the *Just George* exhibition at Stromness Museum in 2006, it isn't part of the museum's permanent collection and its current location seems to be unknown.

There were other interesting objects too, less easy to summon up now, the room's features blurring in my mind with the passage of time: one of them was a whaler's harpoon. When I was trying to find out how George had acquired this, his friend Moira Burgess, a writer who lives in Glasgow, mentioned having discovered a short story by Alex Hamilton, who had visited Orkney and interviewed George.[19] The story relates that Jimmy Isbister, a local man, sold the harpoon to George for half a crown, and Moira had heard tales about Jimmy from George himself. An article by Maurice Fleming in the *Scots Magazine*, also sent to me by Moira, said that Fleming remembered seeing the harpoon at George's house, lying near the fireplace, and being told by George that a friend had come across it at the Stromness rubbish dump.[20]

One of the pictures in George's room was a black-and-white

drawing of Robert Rendall, the Orkney poet and naturalist, walking on the West Shore path near Stromness. Rendall, born in 1898, was a writer whom George knew well and whose work he admired,[21] and the drawing was by the Stromness artist Ian MacInnes, who had been at school with George and was his lifelong friend. Ian was highly regarded in the community, not only for his paintings, but also as a former rector of Stromness Academy. After George died I sometimes thought of the drawing of Rendall and wondered what had become of it, so it was a joy to see it again in 2014 when I visited the home of his friends Brian and Liza Murray at Hoymansquoy in Stromness; it was given to them by George's nephew Erlend Brown.

Another picture which was later displayed above George's fireplace was *Stromness Harbour Front*, also by Ian MacInnes, but this would not have been there when I first went to Mayburn Court. Erlend told me that it originally belonged to John Broom, a friend and sometimes sparring partner of George's; it was especially fitting that George should have it because it showed Clouston's Pier (also known as Clouston's Close), where he was born and where he lived until he was six years old (when the family moved to Melvin Place). In 1993, George wrote about this painting in 'Under Brinkie's Brae', mentioning that it 'used to hang on the wall of John Broom's house in Franklin Road' but adding 'It came to me by way of our mutual friend Paddy Hughes.' He went on to reminisce about living on Clouston's Pier, and ended the piece by saying 'I hope to hang it over the mantelpiece, any day now.'[22]

There were other paintings too in George's house; in the scribbled draft of a poem, I mentioned 'Sylvia's window', referring to a work by the artist Sylvia Wishart, a close friend of George's, but two decades later, trying to summon up this painting, I couldn't remember it at all, in spite of having seen it about twice a week over the course of several years. I thought that the window in question must be the one facing across to Hoy from Sylvia's house at Heatherybraes on the outskirts of Stromness, as the view from that window appears in many of her works, layered with subtle reflections from within the room, but eventually I asked Erlend about it and he directed me to a book published by the Pier Arts Centre, *Sylvia Wishart: A Study*, which includes a reproduction of the painting that I was trying to recall: *From a Window, Rackwick*.[23] Memory plays strange tricks, because I had looked at my copy of this book many times and never recognised that painting as the one I had seen so often in George's house, yet when I checked again, after reading Erlend's email, I could immediately visualise *From a Window* hanging on the wall at Mayburn Court. It wasn't painted at Heatherybraes as I had surmised, but at Sylvia's cottage, North-House, at Rackwick. Erlend knows this house well, 'having stayed there a few times in my youth', and in his email he referred to Rackwick's 'strong influence on both Sylvia & George, and of course Max [Sir Peter Maxwell Davies] too in the 70s & beyond'.[24] The dominant features of the picture are a spray of twigs in a pale jug and an oil lamp on a window sill; through the window, one can see a stretch of golden grass, cliffs, a headland, the sea and an expanse of sky beyond. Mel Gooding's essay in the Pier Arts Centre book says, of 'the Interiors and Lamp paintings', that 'the palette is muted and tonal, greys and ochres, dark to light; bare black branches in the vase suggest winter, the lamp is prepared for the darkness of a long winter night'.[25]

When I visited George in the evenings there was always a coal fire burning – even, I think, in summer. In later years, Brian Murray would come across unfailingly each day from his house in Alfred Terrace which overlooks Mayburn Court, to clear the grate and light the fire. Brian visited Orkney frequently for many years, and he and Liza came to live here permanently in 1991, after his retirement.[26] George would let the room grow dusky, lit only by the flames until daylight had faded almost completely, and I remember a welcome sense of contentment and peace after a busy or difficult day. We would talk for a while in the semi-darkness until George flicked on the Anglepoise lamp beside his chair, and then, in an almost unchanging ritual, he would leave me to contemplate the fire or read a magazine while he disappeared into the small kitchen to make a pot of tea, which he brought into the living room on a tray. Often there would be biscuits and cake as well. The tea would be poured into flowered china cups with saucers – never mugs – and on special occasions or bitter winter nights the tea might be followed by a generous dram. Sometimes, walking home quite late from a reading or a concert, I would see the light of George's lamp or the flickering glow from his fire as I passed Mayburn Court and would knock on his door on impulse to tell him some small piece of news that I thought he might enjoy. In those days I was always greeted affectionately with a hug and a kiss, and he never turned me away.

As we drank our tea or whisky we talked, sometimes for hours – although it was possible, too, not to talk at all but merely to sip our tea in companionable silence as the coals settled in the grate. Our conversation often consisted of the small details of the day – trivial fragments of our lives rather than matters of great national interest or profound truths. But George did tell me many stories about Stromness and its past and present inhabitants, and this helped me to feel less of a stranger in the town. In an unfinished poem I attempted to capture my feeling of privilege and inclusion, explaining how George drew me into a circle of firelight and voices, showing me another world. He described joys and tragedies and intriguing goings-on – marriages, births and deaths; tangled family histories; infidelities and illegitimacies; rows and resentments. I don't remember him ever being malicious about anyone, and many of his tales were extremely funny; Maggie Fergusson refers to George's endearing sense of mischief and his enjoyment of gossip, as recalled by Flora Jack, secretary to Edwin Muir – an Orcadian novelist and poet who was also a warden at Newbattle Abbey College in Edinburgh, where George was a student.[27] It often amazed me that George, who didn't seem to go out very much, apparently knew about almost everything that was happening in the town and far beyond it.

In a rather poor exchange for George's Stromness sagas, I told him about my life in London, my work, my friends, my marriage (I had parted from my first husband, Martin Ramsey, in 1978, though I continued to use his surname) and my past romances, and he always wanted to know what I was doing at the school and to hear about the people I had met recently. In our younger lives we had inhabited contrasting worlds, but many of our values and ideas were not so very different. What I loved most was to hear him speak about his childhood: his memories of playing barefoot on the shore and clambering over the rocks; holidays at a cottage in Stenness; his mother Mhairi's cheerful singing as she worked in the house; his older sister

Ruby, disappointed that baby George wasn't a girl, dressing him in a bonnet and pushing him in the pram, telling the people they passed that he was her little sister.

It was good, too, to hear the latest news from Hopedale and Langskaill, the houses where George regularly visited the Bevans and the Dixons respectively; he had lunch with Archie and Elizabeth Bevan most Fridays, as I recall ('Soup and bread and ale, at Hopedale, / At two o'clock'),[28] and tea with Allison, Fraser and Magnus Dixon on Mondays unless the roads were icy – he had a dread of not being able to get back to his own bed. Fraser used to collect him in the car and drive him to and from Langskaill, not far from Stromness, and was thoughtful in many other ways; he sometimes brought terracotta pots of vivid geraniums to brighten up the balcony outside 3 Mayburn Court. Meeting George opened so many doors for me: far from regarding with suspicion or reserve this incomer who was suddenly spending so much time with him, the people who cared about him – with the exception of Renée Simm – welcomed me with an unanticipated generosity. I was invited to Hopedale for meals with George, and sometimes other guests would be there too, such as Ian and Jean MacInnes, and Dr Derrick Johnstone and his wife Susie. Derrick was not only George's close friend, but also his GP for many years (he retired shortly after I arrived in Orkney and so I was never one of his patients). The Johnstones live just along the road from Archie and Elizabeth, and both houses are a short stroll from Mayburn Court. At Hopedale, a flight of steps leads down from the front door to the street, and across the road lies the sea; I have a vivid memory of standing with George at the top of the steps after dinner on a winter's night, looking at the stars, and the moving lights of cars coming down the Scorradale Road in Orphir, across the water, talking of our hopes for a glimmer of the aurora borealis from the north as we walked home.

Visitors from the mainland, too – such as Brian and Liza Murray, who were based in Ayrshire when I moved to Orkney, and Peter and Betty Grant from Aberdeen (Peter was the City Librarian at that time) – all treated me like an old friend when they came to see George. No one appeared to be in the least bit surprised at this newly sprung friendship between a man in his sixties and a woman more than thirty years younger. George had other women friends, of course. Early on in our acquaintance he mentioned one evening that the flowers I was admiring on his table had been picked by Nora – 'my good friend Nora Kennedy' was how he described her – in her garden in Deerness, in the east mainland of Orkney. He said that she often came on the bus to spend a few days in Stromness and he wanted me to meet her because he was sure that we would like one another. It wasn't long before she was at Mayburn Court again and George was able to introduce us. Luckily we did like one another. She almost always greeted me with kindness and apparent pleasure, and the three of us spent many evenings together.

Nora was in her early fifties then, an attractive dark-haired woman who dressed with care and wore some stylish scarves. She had a tendency towards vagueness – which could be charming or exasperating, depending on the circumstances – and to lateness; I remember her calmly making toast for her breakfast about ten minutes before we were due to leave for a lunchtime concert at the St Magnus Festival. Her obituary in *The Independent* on 29 August 2007, written by Maggie Fergusson, was subtitled 'Muse to George Mackay Brown' and revealed that Nora was born in Vienna in 1936, named Eleonora Berger. She was divorced by the time I met her but she spoke sometimes about her former husband, Donald Kennedy, in a way that made it clear they were still friends. Her affection and respect for George were readily apparent; she was inclined to fuss over him sometimes but it was hard not to be touched by her devotion to him, even without knowing much about the history of their relationship. One September, having some birthday money to spend and wanting to buy a piece of local jewellery, I found a lovely silver and turquoise necklace in the Waterfront Gallery and was astonished when the owner of the gallery, Trudi Hall, told me that Nora had made it – George had never mentioned that she possessed such skill, although he was delighted when I told him about buying the necklace. I wore it to Mayburn Court the next time that Nora was visiting, and she said she was happy to know I had it, paying me a gracious compliment. She also created fine window displays for Trudi and I would occasionally see her standing outside the shop, surveying her work, trying to decide on the perfect place for a piece of pottery or a picture.

Although George and Nora sometimes niggled each other, his continuing fondness for her was plain to see. On one occasion, when he had invited me to spend the evening with them, I arrived to find them watching television, sitting closely together on the sofa and holding hands. They greeted me happily as I came in, both quite at ease, and there was no sense that I was intruding. A perceptive obituary of Nora written by Geoffrey Elborn (who formerly lived in Stromness) claimed that George was 'the love of her life' and suggested that how much she meant to George has perhaps never been made sufficiently clear.[29]

Maggie Fergusson discusses their relationship in George's biography,[30] but Elborn explained that when that book was being written, Nora 'was reluctant to co-operate, believing that her relationship with the writer was a private matter. As a result, her importance in his life was not fully explored.'[31]

In later years, when Nora was seriously ill, her mood was often – and understandably – darker and I felt less sure of her regard, but in those first months of our acquaintance we were at ease with one another, and I was glad of her acceptance of me and her willingness to share George's company. After his death I didn't see her so frequently, partly because she came less often to Stromness and also because there was a sense that without George we no longer had a shared focus and there were fewer things to talk about, but I would never have cut her out of my life. Apparently others did; Elborn suggested that Nora 'was deeply hurt when many of Mackay Brown's friends, ignoring the fact that her friendship with him had enriched his life, severed all contact with her when he died'.[32]

During many of the evenings on which George and I spent time together without other visitors there, our conversation would turn to books – as one might expect, since he was a writer and I was a librarian with a literature degree. We enjoyed discussing what we were reading at the time, or books we had loved in the past: the names that cropped up most often were W. B. Yeats, D. H. Lawrence, Joseph Conrad, Henry James, E. M. Forster, Gerard Manley Hopkins and Thomas Mann. I had read most of these authors fairly widely, but I knew only a little of Mann's work, so George urged me to read *The Magic Mountain* and I fell under its spell. Until I read George's autobiography, I didn't know that he had done postgraduate research on Hopkins – 'Inscape in the Poetry of Hopkins'[33] – but I quickly learned that his poetry held a special power for George: 'I feel that his life and writing was a seeking for the sources of things, from which new life springs perpetually . . . [He] had to throw away the old worn moulds of language, and mint words and images as if they were being used for the first time.'[34] Alain-Fournier's name came up too, as one of my favourite novels then was *Le Grand Meaulnes*, although I had read only an English translation. Alan Bold points out that in one of George's short stories, 'The Eye of the Hurricane',[35] the character Barclay is reading Alain-Fournier's novel and describes it as 'an exquisite rural idyll'. Bold adds that George read *Le Grand Meaulnes* at Edwin Muir's suggestion: 'an interesting book which I think would be completely in your world'.[36]

During these conversations I tried to conceal from George that as far as his own writing was concerned I was still shockingly ignorant. The first book of his that I bought (from Tam MacPhail at Stromness Books & Prints, known to locals for many years as 'Tam's bookshop') was *Time in a Red Coat*[37] – which, I must confess, I found quite difficult – and I put myself on a sort of GMB crash course, bringing his books home from the school library, or reading them at my desk in the lunch-hour if they were precious out-of-print volumes such as *Loaves and Fishes*.[38] Another early purchase was the new edition of *Portrait of Orkney*, from which I learned much about my new surroundings.[39] I was glad to find Alan Bold's book, too, which helped me to understand more about George's work – 'a vast ocean over which shine starlike images and symbols'.[40] With hindsight, I should perhaps have paid more attention to a passage quoted by Bold from George's short story 'The

Drowned Rose' in *Hawkfall*: 'There is a trouble in the islands that is called morbus orcadensis. It is a darkening of the mind, a progressive flawing and thickening of the spirit. It is said to be induced in sensitive people by the long black overhang of winter.'[41] But in those early days I found George almost always cheerful, and had no inkling of the depression that he was so careful to hide from most of his friends.

George's writing seemed to me extraordinary in a number of ways, not least because of its transparent honesty and its directness, which often moved and sometimes perplexed me. It is difficult to describe the impact that his poems, in particular, had on me: they seemed fresh and new, their images and phrasing innovative and at times even daring, and yet I read them with a sense of immediate familiarity, as if I had known them for years. Some words had a compelling simplicity – 'Blessings and soup plates circled'[42] – and certain vivid and beautiful lines would stay in my mind for days, or weeks: for instance, 'The Sound today a burning sapphire bough / Fretted with mimic spring', and 'The sea tears like acres of blue silk'.[43] The rhythm of his stanzas would pound in my head as I paced the West Shore after work or supper, walking in the landscape that had inspired him. I was drawn in, too, by George's powerful use of religious symbols; that aspect of his work appealed to me very much. We rarely talked about religion in the first months of our friendship, but later it became a more frequent topic, although George was always measured and reticent when speaking to me of his beliefs. In recent years I have found Ron Ferguson's book about George's faith and his path to Catholicism to be wonderfully enlightening in that respect.[44]

Friends have sometimes wanted to know whether George talked to me about his work, but with regret I must say that it was quite unusual for us to discuss in any detail whatever it was that he was writing at the time, perhaps partly because although I often longed to ask, I felt wary of intruding too far into that private, creative territory. I had an instinctive sense that this wasn't something he needed or wanted from me – it quickly became apparent that I wasn't going to have that kind of role in his life; nor would I be another of his muses. I might make a few tentative enquiries about whether he felt it had been a good morning for writing, but his replies tended to be evasive, along the lines of 'I'm just trying my hand at a new story.' He hardly ever volunteered any such information, and so I was astonished when he once put a thick, folded wad of paper into my lap and asked me to look at the proofs of *The Wreck of the Archangel* (published in 1989 by John Murray) and to tell him what I thought of the poems. Disappointingly – for myself and possibly also for George – I was almost at a loss for words, insufficiently confident to offer much in the way of comment. Throughout our friendship, and in spite of my affection for the man, I was always rather in awe of the writer.

I wasn't alone in being afraid of trespassing upon George's interior territory. Others, too, have noted that he had his own way of dealing with what he regarded as intrusive questions. There was a certain expression that sometimes fell across his face – a look of slightly pained severity – if one had said or done something of which he couldn't quite approve, or if one ventured into an area which he considered inappropriate or too private. The expression conveyed, better than words ever could, that he really didn't want to discuss that topic now, if indeed ever, and it was an expression that I was anxious to avoid having to see. In spite of the usually relaxed friendliness between us,

George always seemed to possess an essential reserve, and I dreaded to cross unwittingly the invisible barrier that I sensed was there: if I did, there would be a sudden chill in the air and a disconcerting feeling that I had gone too far. Maggie Fergusson quotes the poet Sheenagh Pugh, who visited George briefly in 1993 and thought that he was someone who kept people at arm's length: 'I had the feeling you could spend a lot of time with him and never get closer than he wanted you to, which would not be very close.'[45] I read those words with a nod of recognition; it was often possible to feel close to George – but then, for some inexplicable reason, he would retreat again.

Ron Ferguson, giving a lecture at the Pier Arts Centre in Stromness in 2011, described how George would resort to humming when confronted with a question that he did not want to answer. Ron also mentioned the writer Stewart Conn, who had recalled George humming Beethoven's *Ninth* or reciting Gerard Manley Hopkins in order to fend off unwanted enquiries.[46] I never experienced the Humming or the Reciting, but I certainly saw the Severe Look a few times, and I always quaked before it. And Liza Murray reminded me recently of George's way of dealing with people who patronised him or underestimated his intelligence and knowledge. He would listen patiently, with an inscrutable expression, and then say 'Oh really? How interesting!' (this has become a catchphrase in the Murray family), with an apparent sincerity that might have fooled anyone who didn't know him well.

As well as finding George extraordinary as a writer, I thought he was a remarkable person, not least because he was content with so little in an increasingly materialistic world. The small kitchen, where he wrote each day at a Formica-topped table, had a special kind of charm precisely because it was the place in which he produced such marvellous streams of words – and yet, seen objectively, it was almost pitifully basic. Looking at Gunnie Moberg's photographs at the Orkney Library & Archive in 2014, I was reminded of just how spartan George's kitchen was, as there are several pictures of George crouching down to feed Nora's cat Gypsy there, when he was doing cat-minding duties. The room served his needs, however, both as a place to work and in terms of his domestic arrangements, which were far from elaborate. He could cook simple meals for himself perfectly well and seemed to enjoy doing so, although he loved to be invited out to the homes of his friends and relations and would sometimes take me to the Ferry Inn in Stromness for an early supper – he preferred not to eat late in the evening. He always insisted on paying for both of us and invariably chose herring in oatmeal, urging me to have the same.

Once, when he was coming to Faravel for a meal and I was tentatively suggesting things that he might enjoy eating, he said, 'Oh no, not lasagne. I don't like pasta *at all*', in a tone of absolute finality (I can still hear it). His friend Renée Simm, who had been born in Paris and grew up there, cooked for him most Thursday lunchtimes and often at the weekend, as far as I recall, but I suspect that the menu was unlikely to have included elaborate French dishes, for Renée would have wanted to please George, and his tastes were conservative. Broth, eggs and fish; sausages, stew and mince; or perhaps a good steak pie: these seemed to be his preferences. In 'Under Brinkie's Brae' he once mentioned some soup I had made for him: 'Enjoy, early evening, a pot of soup Joanna brought down. Good broth and a good-going fire, and winter seems OK.'[47]

One icy day in January 1996 he rang me at breakfast time to ask me to get some shopping for him ('a few messages', he would have said), as he sometimes did when the weather was bad. Later, I described the incident in a piece for the *Hoy Sound*:

[I] set out with George's list (and strict instructions to take a note of the cost of everything, for he was meticulous about settling up) and a grumpy toddler. The snow was turning to dirty slush and it was slow-going with the pushchair, except when we skeetered down Porteous Brae. Every now and then we would come to a halt as the pushchair ran aground on a lump of congealed grit. About an hour later, I would climb the slippy Mayburn steps with a bag of sausages, half a pound of mince, firelighters, oranges – George's needs were simple and few – and an even grumpier toddler demanding crisps, to be met at the door by George, full of consternation.

'Oh Jo', he would say, 'I forgot I would need two carrots and an onion.'

Fortunately, Stromness being the place it is, Flett Butcher's van would come to the rescue (they deliver two carrots and an onion as cheerfully as a whole side of beef) and we would not have to brave the slushy street again.[48]

George was well known at E. Flett, the butcher's shop (which is still there in John Street, at the time of writing). He recounted an incident on 6 February: 'Going to pay the butcher, discover I've left my wallet at home. The kind butcher lends me a £10 note out of the till, so I can buy my other messages on the way home. Well, a thing like that couldn't happen in a city shop. Such small acts of consideration bind a community together.'[49]

Writing for the *Hoy Sound*, a year on from the events I was describing, when George was no longer with us, I added: 'This winter, when the phone rings at breakfast, how I wish that I could hear George's voice again, asking about firelighters and sausages.'

One thing that there was never any need to buy was cake, for there were always friends – usually ladies, and I was proud to be one of them – who kept George provided with home-bakes, and he gladly shared these with his guests. In later years, Mrs Moyle, who was one of Surinder Punjya's friends, used to send parcels of fruitcake all the way from England, often accompanied by scarves or sweaters that she knitted for George, although she never met him. George appeared to enjoy attending to his visitors' needs, and most offers of help were politely refused. One of the few times I ever saw him irritable was when Nora tried to take charge as he was making a pot of tea and getting out the cake tins: he peevishly shooed her out of the kitchen. As he busied himself with the kettle and the cups I usually occupied myself by reading something from one of the heaps of papers with which I was sharing the sofa.

The writer Kevin Crossley-Holland, in 'Interrogating Silence', a *Kaleidoscope* programme made after George's death, described this situation perfectly: 'the little front sitting room, stacked with all kinds of stuff, layers of it – you had to elbow it and shove it aside to get a seat at all on the rather decrepit sofa in front of the fire'.[50] George once described himself as living 'for years in a wilderness of paper, that has been getting wilder and wilder',[51] and writing in the mid-1990s he remembered that 'People who visited this house in the seventies and eighties remarked on the chaos of books everywhere – as if a literary volcano had erupted and deposited tomes and volumes and pamphlets everywhere, in tottering stacks and strata.'[52]

So there I would sit, with *The Listener* or *The Tablet* or the *Radio Times*, and as I read, if I was lucky, I would hear George singing as he made the tea. It has become one of my dearest, most enduring memories of him – his wavering but quite tuneful voice, filtering through the open kitchen door. The song was usually a hymn, and most often 'Guide Me O Thou Great Redeemer' (by William Williams, with the well-known lines 'Bread of heaven, bread of heaven / Feed me now and evermore', sung to the tune 'Cwm Rhondda' by John Hughes), which I can never hear now without emotion. He told me that his mother always sang as she went about her work; he often spoke of her with great love and admiration. When I was once expressing sympathy for a woman of my acquaintance who had four young children and seemed perpetually busy and tired, George pointed out – or 'retorted' might be a more apt word – that his mother had brought up five children on very little money and without a washing machine or any of the modern aids to domestic life. George himself did have some help from the kind and capable Margaret Laurensen. It must have been difficult to clean around the piles of books and papers, but the room always looked cosy and hospitable: the fire leaping in the grate; the Anglepoise lamp casting its cone of light; the flowers, brought by Nora, drooping gracefully in a vase.

During my first two months in Orkney I gradually got used to the long, light nights of June and July, but August brought with it an almost autumnal feel: 'Moon roundly brilliant; stars out; the cold black, coal-black sea slapping and plucking at the nousts', I wrote in a notebook.[53] 'The *Sunniva* decked out with lights, safely home at the pier; the red beacon flashes out across the water, which is never still.' In September I went to Rackwick for the first time, knowing that it was a special place for George and wanting to see it for myself. I had been across to Hoy twice already, during my sister Jen's visit and again at the end of August, but both those trips were on evening sailings of the MV *Jessie Ellen* (the passenger ferry that went between Stromness and Hoy, now replaced by the MV *Graemsay*). This later crossing meant that people could have dinner at the Hoy Inn and return the same night, but there was little time left for exploring. George had spoken to me about his love for Rackwick, and about Dorothy and Jack Rendall and their daughter Lucy, who lived at Glen, and about Sir Peter Maxwell Davies (known to George, and later to me, as 'Max'), who owned the cottage called Bunertoon and found inspiration for his music there.

None of these conversations had quite prepared me for the first glimpse of that 'green bowl gently tilted between the hills and ocean'[54] and its remarkable if austere beauty. I walked up from Moaness pier, past the small loch where great skuas swooped overhead, and then through the long valley, eventually catching sight of light shining on the sea between headlands. I searched in vain for the right words to capture that view, acknowledging later 'the truth of GMB's belief that the language is worn out, metaphors exhausted, the descriptive words having long since lost their freshness & innocence'. Writing about Rackwick in his autobiography, George recalled that a 'lasting spell was cast on me that Sunday as we sat on the grass with our sandwiches and tea, and heard the slow boom of sea on stones and sand, and saw the two immense sea cliffs that guarded the valley'.[55] Even if I couldn't find the words to describe my impressions, I was similarly affected by Rackwick's magic on that September day. On later visits I sensed a different, darker atmosphere – perhaps influenced by having read, in *An Orkney Tapestry*, the terrible story of the boys who drowned in the burn there in 1952 – but on that first occasion there was only a sense of joy. 'The sea flies up in a cloud of spray & spume which drifts inland like pale smoke over the green mouth of the valley', I wrote as I sat on the beach. 'And all the time, over it all, even on this fine day, the sea crashes & roars; the wind flickers ceaselessly in spite of the sun's warmth . . . I am happy.'

I saw George during the week following my trip to Hoy, when he came to visit the Academy library for the launch of an educational package, *Bookmaking: A Case Study of Publishing*, which had Orkney connections.[56] Naomi Mitchison's novel *Early in Orcadia* – inspired by a visit to the Tomb of the Eagles on South Ronaldsay – had been chosen by the Scottish Film Council as a focus for the pack, and there was also an important link with our town: 'The Stromness connection is a strong one. Not only is the package centred on the book, which is about the prehistoric past of Orkney, but it contains considerable input from Mr George Mackay Brown, the well-known poet and author.'[57] Sadly, Lady Mitchison, ninety-one years old at the time, was not able to attend the launch because she was away 'in Botswana for a spell doing her duty as a tribal mother'. She had a long connection with Botswana, as her own writing demonstrates, and I was delighted to find – in an essay she wrote in 1963 – this intriguing statement: 'I am now tribal adviser to the Bakgatla, a job which has its similarities with being County

Councillor for Kintyre East.'[58] Her absence in Stromness that day was much regretted, but a photograph accompanying the article in *The Orcadian* showed George standing amidst a gathering of pupils and local dignitaries, his spectacles shining in the light of the camera's flashbulb.

I didn't see George the following weekend because I was in Glasgow for a few days, staying with friends. On the afternoon that I flew back to Orkney, Elaine Gordon met me at the airport and took me to her house for tea before driving me home to Stromness, and I went down to Mayburn Court that evening, anxious to see George again. He came to Faravel on 17 September, the day before my thirty-sixth birthday:

[I] never could have dreamed that I'd be spending it beside the sea in this sublime Northern place ... silvered light streams through a grey sky ... the house is warm; the cat peacefully asleep. Last night George was here, for supper (fish pie and baked bananas), bringing *Three Plays* (inscribed with 'Love, George'), a birthday song for me, & a record of Yeats's poetry, to which we listened after the meal whilst Billie slept beside him on the sofa, & he said, 'She's a real honey of a cat.'

The three plays were *The Loom of Light*, *The Well* and *The Voyage of Saint Brandon*,[59] and the birthday song was an acrostic – one of a number that he wrote for me, as he did for many of his friends and relations. I know he must have produced hundreds of these over the years, but that didn't make mine any less precious:

Just before the equinox, and before farmers set up
Oat-stooks, barley-stooks,
Abundant gold of summer, on Orkney hills,
Now we must welcome
Newcomers to our fires and tables,
And especially Joanna – may she bide long! –
                              on her birthday.

I saw George again a few days after this, on 22 September – a letter to my parents mentions 'a drink at George's' – and he appears here and there in my rather disjointed account of the autumn, which most often describes walks and weather: 'Warebeth – the tide far out & the beach deserted, marked only by one set of human prints & the deeper marks of a horse . . . I lay on the bed & the cat came & sat uncertainly on the curve of my hip, & the rain fell outside.'

During the first week of October, one of my nephews, Andrew, was staying with me and this happened to be during the making of the film *Venus Peter*, so we drove out to Dingieshowe beach one night to see a model whale that had been specially made for the film.[60] Andrew set off on his long journey home to Kent on 8 October, and that night I went with George to Archie Bevan's retirement dinner at the Stromness Hotel, which was a happy and lively occasion. I was at Mayburn Court for the evening on the 11th, and two days later I was invited to Elizabeth and Archie's house, again with George, before leaving the following day on the MV *St Sunniva* to visit my parents. Although I very much wanted to see them, I found it hard to tear myself away from Orkney: 'mist over Orphir early, low down by the shore but leaving the hills more clearly etched;

then the sun gaining strength so that when I walked back . . .
& turned up Hellihole Road, there was blue sky in patches &
the soft smell & moist light of a day in early spring, rather than
October at the summer's turn'.

I was sad to be missing George's birthday on 17 October,
having to make do with talking to him on the phone from
hundreds of miles away, but I was back in time for a reading
by Norman MacCaig at the Pier Arts Centre later that month,
to which both George and I had been looking forward. There
was also a special television programme to watch together at the
end of October, as the chef Keith Floyd had visited Orkney that
summer. George and the Grants were staying at Rackwick when
a BBC television crew arrived with Floyd to film a local resident
making Partan Bree (crab soup) – 'in the house right beside us',
George reported in 'Under Brinkie's Brae'.[61] A brief article later
that year, at the time of the programme's transmission, noted
that 'Mr David Hutchison of Hoy will demonstrate the art of
soup-making in a kitchen which he is said to have made largely
from old fish boxes washed up on the beach.'[62] The crew had
filmed several other Orkney people too, including Alan Craigie
at the Creel Restaurant as he made Cullen Skink, a fish soup.
A photograph of Floyd in Orkney, standing on what appears
to be the deck of a rusting blockship, was used to illustrate his
obituary in *The Guardian* in 2009.

I saw George several times in November, but it was a busy
month and my notebook was neglected: 'Wrote nothing – out
of busy-ness & apathy . . . winter sunrises . . . Dave Kirkland
ringing to say the Northern Lights were in the sky – evenings
with Alison – meetings with George – making the acquaintance
of Jim Lawson . . . Accepted & surrounded by friendly faces.' (I

had met Dave and his wife Donella on my first visit to Orkney, and Jim was one of my colleagues at the Academy.)

Meanwhile, George had been enjoying the company of his 'Ayrshire friend Brian Murray', who was visiting Orkney again. In 'Under Brinkie's Brae' he explained that Brian 'must not be designated as "from Ayrshire" any longer, as he owns a house in Alfred Terrace now'. Going on to remark on the wind that had been 'howling' for several days, George wistfully remembered the 'jewelled beauty' of the weather on the previous Saturday and mentioned having met Sinéad Cusack, one of the leading actors in *Venus Peter*, who 'had walked among the hills that afternoon and had lain among the heather in the sun, and it was, she said, "pure enchantment" '.[63] He enjoyed telling me the story of how he heard a knock on the door quite late on that Saturday night and opened it to find Sinéad Cusack in the company of a local man, James Budge, whom George knew well – they made a rather incongruous couple. James had met the actor in one of the Stromness pubs, and when he discovered that she was interested in meeting George he was happy to oblige by taking her along to Mayburn Court. I asked James recently about this story and he confirmed that it was accurate, mentioning that by chance he had also met Sinéad Cusack's father, Cyril Cusack, when he visited Orkney some years earlier.

At the beginning of December, George and I were at another book launch, and this time I was invited as his guest. I described the event in a letter to my parents, telling them that it was 'the nicest evening I'd had for a while'. The book in question was *Shoal and Sheaf*,[64] a collection of archive photographs of Orkney, for which George had written the introduction – the title was taken from *An Orkney Tapestry*: 'Yet now we are glad / For all things turn to the sun. / Our hands reach across light from shoal to sheaf.'[65] One of the photographs showed the demolition of the Stromness distillery, and the Mayburn Court houses were later built on that site, but they were not, as has been suggested elsewhere, a conversion of the distillery.[66] George asked me to go to Mayburn Court first for a dram to set us up for the evening, and then Erlend Brown – who was at that time the curator of the Pier Arts Centre – drove us into Kirkwall. It was quite a formal occasion and there were several speeches, including one by the convenor of Orkney Islands Council, but George appeared to enjoy it, especially being able to chat to people whom he seldom saw. I couldn't help noticing with mild amusement that as George's guest – both at this event and at Archie Bevan's retirement dinner – I was treated with particular courtesy, as if being his companion entitled me to special treatment. George, whilst behaving impeccably, was entirely without pretensions – he disliked too much formality and fuss.

As soon as this part of the evening was over we had to hurry back to Stromness for the opening of the annual Christmas exhibition at the Pier Arts Centre. This was an altogether more relaxed affair, with hot punch and mince pies and many good pictures to look at, if one could squeeze through the throng of people. During the drive from Kirkwall, Erlend mentioned that the Australian artist Sir Sidney Nolan was having an exhibition at the Pier the following summer and would himself be coming to Stromness, and this news was of great interest to me.[67] I first came across Nolan's work through friends from university days and was excited to think that I might have the opportunity to meet him. I mentioned this in a letter to my parents, together with the fact that I had seen 'P. Maxwell Davies in the doorway of the delicatessen' a few days previously; I thought my father would enjoy teasing me about this shameless bit of name-dropping, as indeed he did.

Alison Blacklock was also at the Pier's private view. She and her two young sons lived in a flat a few doors away from the gallery, and when people began to drift away at the end of the evening she asked if George and I would like to go back to have coffee. I thought perhaps George might be tired but he accepted with alacrity. It was a memorable night, worth noting in the diary: 'A dram with George and then Erlend taking us to the book launch. The drive back, in the dark, discussing Nolan. Then the Pier. Coffee at Alison's – such a lovely happy evening. And walking home along the street from Alison's, with George. He kissed me, at the corner of Mayburn Court.' It was a warm kiss on the lips, as always – but not a passionate kiss. I was never romantically involved with George, although I loved him dearly and I believe that he loved me too, in his own way. From the very beginning there was a sense of inevitability about our friendship, and all through my first winter in Orkney a feeling of underlying familiarity persisted – that this was where I was meant to be: 'the black windy darkness . . . the slap of the sea at the piers a voice I seem always to have heard', I wrote. 'Lamplit squares behind curtains make the darkness friendly.'

Further into December, the weather became more violent; I walked to Warebeth beach in a gale, 'which through the campsite was as tangible as a hand against my back, forcing me on . . . Ward Hill – menacing dark with gold lights, like lamps seen through smoke.' After being out on such a wild day it was soothing to go to Mayburn Court in the evening and sit with George – and sometimes with Nora (who was there on 4 December) – talking by the fire or watching television while the wind howled outside. In those days George enjoyed all sorts of programmes (I always had to be careful not to arrive in the middle of a football match, in order to avoid the Severe Look) and he would mark in the *Radio Times* the ones he particularly wanted to watch. Moira Burgess remembers that he liked *Countdown*, a game show on Channel 4, 'in its Richard Whiteley days, finding it good-natured and gentle', and she also recalls a 'truly surreal' conversation with George about a Ben Elton programme that they had both seen.[68] When he wandered off to the kitchen to make tea, he would often suggest that I should take note of his choices – 'A good play on Wednesday, Jo, don't miss that.'

Details of some of the programmes that we saw together have blurred a little. I have a vivid memory of one particularly happy evening that seemed to date from 1990, watching a powerful monologue performance by Fiona Shaw, whom George greatly admired, but when researching details I found that the film I recalled was Deborah Warner's production of T. S. Eliot's *The Wasteland*,[69] which wasn't shown on television until December 1995. A film that I did see in December 1990, and almost certainly with George at Mayburn Court, was *My Left Foot*, directed by Jim Sheridan in 1989, with Daniel Day-Lewis in the leading role and Fiona Shaw playing the part of Dr Eileen Cole. It told the true story of Christy Brown, the Irish writer and painter who had cerebral palsy and who was able to write or type only with the toes of one foot. George would have had a particular interest in the story, as one of his own great-nephews, David Dixon, has cerebral palsy – Ron Ferguson's book refers to George's 'special affection' for David, who gained a First in English at Edinburgh University and went on to do post-graduate research.[70]

I have another memory, of a programme that I watched with George at Hopedale after dinner with Archie and Elizabeth and other guests: *W. B. Yeats: Cast a Cold Eye*. The clearest thing is a sense of being inspired – not only by the poetry of Yeats, which I had loved for years, but also by the subsequent conversation about it – and finding words and phrases tumbling through my head, and wanting to get home so that I could write them down before I lost them.

On the day after the book launch in Kirkwall, George rang to ask me to go to Mayburn Court to watch an adaptation of D. H. Lawrence's novel *The Rainbow* – a favourite of mine – directed by Stuart Burge, with Imogen Stubbs playing the part of Ursula Brangwen. It was mischievous of George to invite me, because he knew full well that Renée Simm would be there that night. He always tried to ensure that Renée and Nora were never in his house at the same time, since the fur would be likely to fly; Maggie Fergusson mentions that 'the atmosphere tended to be strained' when Renée and Nora were both at Mayburn Court and that 'George did his best to keep them apart.'[71] Yet he would sometimes ask me to call in when he knew perfectly well that Renée was planning to be there, and I wondered whether this was because he was amused by our half-hearted attempts to be civil to one another. When Surinder moved to Stromness, Renée took such a liking to him that she was willing to share George, but that did not appear to be the case with Nora or with me. On the evening of *The Rainbow*, George's rather lame excuse for inviting me as well as Renée was that it would be 'less embarrassing' for him if I were there too. There were sure to be some steamy scenes of which Renée would disapprove, and he claimed that he would feel more comfortable with a third person present. That sounded a bit dubious to me and certainly I found the evening awkward, to say the least (when talking to Ron Ferguson, who came to interview me for his book about George, I used the word 'excruciating'[72]), and I was glad that we were sitting in the firelight and could not clearly see each other's faces.

Somehow we got through it, and later I wrote: 'At George's tonight, I watched *The Rainbow* & was moved almost to tears . . . I had dreaded this adaptation, but it was true to the essentials.' As we watched, I glanced across at Renée from time to time; I thought that she looked rather disapproving but she did not make disparaging comments as I had feared she might. I can still visualise her, sitting very upright, her white hair wound into a knot, dressed in the sombre colours that seemed to be her usual attire, somehow faintly Dickensian. Looking recently at two photographs of her, I was surprised to see that she is wearing a blue patterned blouse in one of them, and a light blue blouse under a darker pinafore dress in the other – in my memories she was always in black, with one exception. After George died, she invited me once to her house and I was astonished when she appeared in an emerald-green tracksuit.

One of my last outings with George in 1988 was to the Pier Arts Centre for the Foy on 9 December, an Orkney Arts Society event organised by Alistair Peebles, who taught English at Stromness Academy. George agreed to write a review:

Four of the younger generation of Orkney poets read a selection of their work to a crowded audience . . . John Aberdein,

Pam Beasant, Debbie Godding, and Fiona MacInnes . . . a felicitous mingling of different styles . . . a delightful way to spend a winter evening. We were reminded over and over that this is how poetry should be, not vague romantic mooning over pretty things, but a full confrontation with life, in all its immediacy and wonder and suffering . . .

He gave careful consideration to each of the participants and their work:

the committed down-to-earth verse of John Aberdein, of whom Brecht would have been proud; the meditative verse of Pam Beasant, including a vivid moving elegy on her father; the wide range and sweep of Debbie Godding, with beautiful descriptions of the countryside . . . and Fiona MacInnes whose inspiration comes from her own surroundings in Orkney, and vivid lyrical childhood memories.[73]

He went on to comment more minutely on the pieces that were read, and it is characteristic of George that he should pay such sensitive attention to the work of others, generously giving praise and encouragement. Even the programme, which I designed, got a mention: 'that could well be, in time, a collector's piece'. We were all very impressed to learn that a collection of Debbie's poetry would shortly be published by Bloodaxe Books (*The Sin Eater*, by Deborah Randell), and it was reviewed in the *Orcadian* the following May.

George and I had dinner together at Archie and Elizabeth's on Sunday 11 December, and on the following Sunday he came up to Faravel to have an evening meal with me – Orkney beef in red wine, followed by some kind of pudding and glasses of Laphroaig. For years I had the impression that George loved puddings and I often made them for him, but Moira Burgess recently found a cutting from *The Glasgow Herald*, dated April 1988,[74] in which George claimed that he was 'not fond of desserts' and preferred to end his meal with stewed or fresh fruit. Moira joked that my puddings must have converted him, but it's more likely that he ate them uncomplainingly in order to spare my feelings, although he did say in 'Under Brinkie's Brae' that when he was in hospital and not allowed to eat, he was 'thinking all the time about sausages and eggs . . . and apple pie'.[75] After dinner that evening, Billie the cat sat on George's lap as we talked for a while. He had brought gifts for me: one was a signed copy of *Magnus* and I remember thinking that he must surely have noticed on his previous visits to my house that I didn't have my own copies of most of his books. He also brought an LP, *The Orcadian Poet George Mackay Brown Reads his Poems and a Story*, recorded by Ioan Allen in Orkney in July 1971 and produced by Claddagh Records. The cover incorporates four striking photographs by Jeffrey Craig: George at the Ring of Brodgar; two pictures of the Earl's Palace in Kirkwall; and a portrait study of George smoking a pipe, looking worried and severe.

I couldn't have foreseen then how much I would value this gift after his death; to be able to hear his voice again was painful and yet consoling. George brought a card as well, that evening, and in my collection of memorabilia I have eight beautiful Christmas cards from him, seven of which comprise a seasonal poem by George, illustrated by his friend Simon Fraser. The eighth card, the last that George sent to me, features his poem

'Lux Perpetua', written for Surinder at the time of his father's death.[76]

George came again to Faravel on Christmas Eve, bringing Nora with him; she was staying at Mayburn Court and they were going to Langskaill together the following day to have their Christmas dinner with the Dixons and Renée. I was to have mine with Alison Blacklock and her two sons, my parents having been heroically understanding about my desire to be in Orkney this Christmas. I had dinner with George on the evening of 30 December, and we parted with hugs and kisses and looked forward to seeing each other in the New Year.

2

A WIDENING CIRCLE

There was a party at Hopedale on 2 January 1989, and Archie and Elizabeth Bevan had asked me to go along. It was quite late when I arrived and the house was already a throng of people, full of light and the sound of voices and the delicious smells of food. Massive saucepans of chilli and rice prepared by Elizabeth stood simmering on the stove, and drink flowed generously. 'George has been asking for you', someone said, leading me through the crowded rooms to where George sat, animated and happy, drinking Archie's famous home brew, and pulling up a chair for me beside him. It was a marvellous beginning to the year and it is a pity that I was too busy to keep an account of everything else that was happening. All I have is this rather disappointing record:

I have written nothing since before Christmas. And someday must set down all the extraordinary events of the intervening time . . . the evening George came here to dinner alone, & said, upon leaving, that it was one of the happiest evenings of the whole year . . . and George and Nora came on Christmas

Eve . . . and then there were two days with the sheep . . . a
brief visit to George . . . New Year at Alison's & the poignant
sound of the ships . . . and Archie & Elizabeth's – sitting
with George . . . the dinner with George here.

The phrase 'two days with the sheep' referred to my attempts to
give a helping hand to a friend in Stenness. Clad in an oilskin
and a layer of mud, I soothed the sheep and held them still
while she attended to their feet, and I looked forward to telling
George about it when I next saw him. At the end of a long
day in the open air, I sat having supper in my friend's slightly
chaotic kitchen, where a cat jumped up on the table and tried
to drink out of the milk jug (on another occasion there were
caddy lambs running in and out as we ate), and thought of
some of the London dinner parties at which I had been a guest,
reflecting contentedly that I felt much more at home here.

An article in *The Orcadian* gave a glimpse of George's
thoughts at that time, as he was one of eight people invited
to express their hopes and aspirations for the coming year.[1]
A photograph accompanying the piece showed him smiling
benignly; above him was a picture of Marjorie Linklater, a
woman of some importance, and Orcadians might be interested
to know that Marjorie's great hope for 1989 was 'for the removal
of the BP oil-tanks from Harbour Road, Kirkwall', for which
many people continued to hope, for many years. Marjorie was
a remarkable person, perhaps too often defined as either the
wife of the writer Eric Linklater or the mother of an editor of
The Scotsman, Magnus Linklater. She was politically active and
deeply involved in many aspects of Orkney life, including the
Orkney Heritage Society, the St Magnus Festival and the Pier

Arts Centre.[2] She lived in Kirkwall and I sometimes met her there; she was always elegant and well dressed, quite often riding her bicycle (even in her last years), and I remember thinking that I would like to age as gracefully as Marjorie.

In his part of the *Orcadian* article, George wished for peace and for the continuing beauty and uniqueness of Stromness, which he feared might go 'under in a wash of grayness [sic] that has been inundating the whole world in the past century'. He hoped for the continuing presence of tourists, 'but not too many . . . May the farmers, the fishermen and the ships never leave us.' On a personal note, he added that he no longer made resolutions, 'knowing what broken shards will lie about me by the end of February. I'll be sorry to miss my breakfast egg, lightly boiled . . . Otherwise I will eat and drink, I hope in moderation, what I like. And may I have the strength of will, at the end of a hard-working day, to switch off dull TV programmes.'

George's friend John Broom was another of the contributors, and his admirable hope was for 'The abolition of *all* weapons of destruction by every nation', although his personal aspiration was more eccentric and humorous: 'To play *Lear* at the Old Vic and to spend a night of passion with Mary Whitehouse' – an activist who vehemently opposed social liberalism and the growth of what became known as 'the permissive society' (a phrase which I heard George himself use occasionally).

After the social whirl of New Year, life settled back into its customary pattern. George explained in a letter to his friend Moira Burgess that 'for the past fortnight any kind of writing has been next to impossible, with visitors & visiting, parties, huge dinners and oceans of drink (nowadays I only paddle in the latter but even so I'm sick of the taste of whisky). I long to get down to work again.'³ His name appears frequently in my scribbled account of January. I visited him a few days after the evening at Archie and Elizabeth's, and on the 15th, which was 'too wild & wet even for me to want to go to the shore', I made an Irish apple cake and took it down to Mayburn Court:

> Home quite late after an evening with George – apart from the usual Stromness gossip, we discussed Tarkovsky, as I had urged him to watch *Ivan's Childhood* last night. And I thought, as before, after our early conversation about Yeats & Hopkins, how fortunate I am to have found George in this place – the unexpected joy of a kindred spirit – someone who will share the beauty of Tarkovsky's extraordinary images.

I had already told George about my mild obsession with the work of the exiled Russian film director Andrei Tarkovsky. Several of his films were being screened that season, including my favourite, *Nostalghia* (1983), and also *Ivan's Childhood* (1962) – an early work that has been widely admired – which I thought that George would like. Ingmar Bergman is quoted as saying that his own discovery of Tarkovsky's early films seemed to him like a miracle: 'Suddenly, I found myself standing at the door of a room, the keys of which had, until then, never been given to me. It was a room I had always wanted to enter and where he was moving freely and fully at ease.'⁴ I felt instinctively that there was a connection between the style of the film and the simplicity and purity of many of the recurring images in George's work, particularly his poetry, and when he talked to me about the film afterwards I knew that my instinct had been right. He recognised and empathised with the qualities that I loved in Tarkovsky, just as I loved them in George's own work.

My diary entry continued:

[George] had been up at John Cumming's house today, with John Aberdein & Pam Beasant & Debbie Godding, to discuss a folio of poems and drawings; a limited edition of 30, priced at £80.

This folio, *Poetry and Poems from Orkney: Cold Kye, Curlew Cry*, published in 1989 by Soulisquoy Press, was the result of a collaboration between several artists and writers in Orkney. George's poem about Brodgar was illustrated by Erlend Brown, and poems by the other writers were illustrated by John Cumming (a Shetland man, the principal teacher of art at Stromness Academy at that time), Jeremy Baster and Christina Smith. John, Pam and Debbie had all read at the Christmas Foy in 1988, and George was happy to join them in working on this project.

Following on from this conversation about the meeting at the Cummings' house, George told me that one of the topics of discussion, as well as the folio itself, had been 'the Born Agains' – by which he meant the Orkney Christian Fellowship. George and I talked about the Fellowship and about the possibility of healing by the laying on of hands, which seemed to interest him very much, although he had other less favourable things to say about charismatic Christianity in general.

I saw George again the following week when he came to dinner at Faravel, and I also invited one of the art teachers from the Academy, Lesley Johns, whom George had known for many years. My notebook from that period records images and impressions of Stromness, with George's name cropping up here and there:

A few clothes blowing on a makeshift line, tied between the prow of a small boat, hauled up on the slipway at the corner by Erlend's house, and a drainpipe on the wall of the Northern Lighthouse Board buildings. A strong wind pushing clouds into a high blue sky, flapping the clothes.

Looking through Stromness windows: a bird hopping in its cage; a geranium. And through Calum's window: a mirror, catching the street's sun; a book lying.

The morning bus to Kirkwall: at the narrow curve by Flett the Butcher, an old man gets on; and up the road, by the fire station, lies a heap of boxes & bruck⁵ – an old adding machine, an old radio, pieces of brass – a lamp, perhaps. The driver helps load it into the back of the bus, & on we go, the journey broken by more passengers than usual, waiting on corners, sheltering by walls. Girls from the school; shy smiles. A mass of crocuses & snowdrops under the trees before the swimming pool. A taste of Spring in wind & sky. The man gets off at Finstown's junk shop . . .

Riding back: a flock of large dark birds motionless in a field . . .

And George rang. Now I must go to Alison's. And back in a gale. A lovely evening, blethering. Home late – George's light still on & I wonder if I should have called in – but the back of half eleven. And tired from the wind.

I did see George, however, on the following evening, and he was eager to regale me with more local news: 'Stromness stories,

"Stromness" people', I wrote, using quote marks because although some of them lived there, or nearby, they were not native Stromnessians. 'George's friend, formerly Elizabeth Gore-Langton . . . who has a cottage – Garth? – up behind Feolquoy, has become the Countess Temple of Stowe.' George enjoyed impressing me with this piece of information, although I think that in general he was unfazed by titles or rank. He was very fond of Elizabeth and had already told me about her love of poetry: many poets who visited Orkney were offered hospitality at Garth, and George recounted a memorable anecdote about Elizabeth hurrying after Ted Hughes in the street, trying to tempt him with the offer of good fishing at Skaill Loch. He mentioned some of this in 'Under Brinkie's Brae' the following year:

> The Festival has been fortunate in its choice of poets, a succession of illustrious bards, beginning with the veteran Norman MacCaig . . .
>
> Some of those poets stayed at Garth, the highest cottage on the Mainland, hospitably looked after by Grenville and Elizabeth Gore-Langton (now Earl and Countess Temple of Stowe). Looking out over Hoy Sound and the open Atlantic, those poets must have thought Orkney an unforgettable place indeed . . .
>
> Ted Hughes fished the lochs, conducted by a man (Dave Brock) who knows the Orkney lochs and all the subtleties of trout, but alas! they were unlucky.[6]

Another story from that evening was about an outbuilding at Garth which Elizabeth's husband Grenville had designated as a 'poetry-free zone', and this amused George immensely. He went on to speak about 'Beverley Smith [now Beverley Ballin Smith], the archaeologist, [who] lives in the other cottage, the one . . . I saw from the top of the Black Craig – & the lovely garden', and among the other names mentioned were Sigrid Mavor (now Sigrid Appleby), who was a friend of Gunnie's; and Mary Peace, whom George sometimes referred to as Mary Moore – I met her at Mayburn Court one evening soon after this, when she called to see George and brought him a bunch of daffodils. He passed on all kinds of interesting snippets of information about people and eventually I began to wonder if there was anyone at all in the islands whose history was unknown to him. He talked about Gunnie being away just then, and did an imitation of Nuff (Tam and Gunnie's dog, of whom I was slightly afraid) coming up to him in the street and gazing imploringly at him as if to say '*Please*, George, can you tell me where Gunnie is? What have they done with her?' This led on to tales about different pets that had belonged to Tam and Gunnie and to his other friends, and I recorded fragments of his narrative:

And George remembered Tiny's kittens – Gunnie stroking Tiny, three days after they'd moved house, & finding her hand wet with milk – driving back to . . . Birsay & finding the kittens still alive – Gypsy & Fankle & others . . .

Fankle used to eat anything, climb on the breakfast table, finish off someone's fried egg. He went for walks along the shore with Archie – was found once at the Town House, sitting [on] someone's desk – another time [in] the Headmaster's study.

To that entry on 29 January I added: 'Evening with GMB a slightly muted pleasure because of my tiredness – but all the customary welcome and affection. Nora is back ... A poet rang – Gerry Cambridge – young & – George thinks – very talented.' When I eventually submitted some poems of my own to the literary magazine *Dark Horse* in 2000, I was pleased to find that it was Gerry who replied (gently rejecting my work) in his role as editor. In our subsequent brief correspondence, he wrote that visits to Orkney simply weren't the same without George there, and that George was the first 'recognised poet' to actively encourage and advise him – 'I owe him a special debt.'[7] Gerry told me that he had written a piece about George that had appeared in *Chapman*, and offered to send me a copy.

On a cold evening at the beginning of February I went down to Mayburn Court to say goodbye to George because I was leaving Orkney the following morning for a short trip to London. He had said that I must be sure not to go away without seeing him, but I found that he already had a visitor – Renée Simm. The conversation between the three of us was general and rather stilted, and after a while I made my escape. George came out into the small unlit hallway, wishing me a safe journey, and we exchanged a hug and our customary kisses. The door to the living room was ajar and I was aware of Renée sitting there, waiting to reclaim George's attention as soon as I had gone. He discreetly pressed a brown envelope into my hand as I left, and I tore it open as I walked up the path between his house and mine, attempting to read the words on the enclosed sheet of paper, but in the darkness of a winter's night I couldn't make them out.

Back at Faravel, standing just inside the kitchen door and still wearing my coat, I read the poem that he had written for me, the one beginning 'How comes this, Joanna?' that is reproduced in the introduction to this book,[8] and he had added a postscript at the bottom of the small piece of deckle-edged paper: 'But don't *you* have a drab weekend, Joanna – Love, George X'. I had known him for just a short time but already he had become an important part of my life, and now I was happy to believe that perhaps the feeling was mutual. I rang him at once to thank him, and there were tears in my eyes as I told him how much his affectionate words meant to me. The imagery of the poem is striking and beautiful, with its emphasis on brightness and fragrance, but it was only years later that I realised, when reading Maggie Fergusson's biography of George, that he had used such imagery more than once before. 'Describing the effect that Kenna's visit had had on him', Fergusson explains, 'George uses precisely the same vocabulary he had used in writing about Stella [Cartwright]: Kenna had "brought a radiance" with her to Orkney, and "left a rare sweetness and fragrance behind" '.[9]

Before I went to bed I wrote a few words about the evening: 'George's – longing to talk to him – heart sinking as I saw Renée there – his giving me the poem as I left – I rang back to thank him.' Next morning I went off to London, leaving George to his 'drab weekend' and although I had a happy and busy time I missed him, and I found that I missed Orkney too: 'I longed, ached, for Warebeth, homesick for my so-recent home.'

I saw George again as soon as I got back. 'Last night: Nora and George', I wrote on 8 February, and added: 'Nora brave.' She said nothing to me about how ill she was, but George told me that she had cancer, sharing his concern with me when she was out of the room. He was often deeply worried about her, in all sorts of ways: about the treatment she needed for her illness; about her constant lack of money; about her efforts to learn to drive so that she wouldn't be so isolated in Deerness. At some point he discovered that she had driven the car alone – perhaps on several occasions – before she had passed her test, and when he told me about this he was clearly exasperated with her because of it, as well as being beside himself with anxiety about what might happen to her if such expeditions became common knowledge.

On that particular evening in February, the three of us sat and watched television together, trying to be cheerful. 'Alan Bennett monologue play: *A Chip in the Sugar*', I noted (it was part of the wonderful *Talking Heads* series, and Stuart Burge directed it), but with no hint of what George had thought of it, and then 'Paul mentioned for the first time.' This referred to the shocking death of a thirteen-year-old pupil at the Academy, Paul Bean, who had gone missing on 27 December after going out to fill a container of peats from a shed at the back of the family house in Birsay. *The Orcadian* reported each week on the searches that were taking place, but Paul had not been seen again until his body was found washed up on the Birsay shore. I knew him slightly because he sometimes came into the Academy library. 'A sense of: this cannot really be so', I wrote. 'Slow dawning painful realisation that it is now too late.' On my walks along the beach and up the Black Craig I had hoped and dreaded to find him – hoping that he would be alive and hiding somewhere, and dreading that I would come across his body. George would certainly have read the reports in the newspaper, but I had been hesitant about raising the troubling subject with him. 'This is unbearable', I added in my notebook.

The boy's fate haunted me, and eventually I wrote a poem based loosely on his story.[10]

On 9 February, Sigrid Mavor invited me to have a meal with her at one of the 'Double Houses' (as they are known locally) in Ness Road, where she was staying for a while. It was Tam and Gunnie's home but they were away at the time and Sigrid was there to look after Nuff. She asked Beverley Smith along too, so that we could get to know one another better. 'Dinner at Sigrid's', I wrote afterwards, 'Beverley also. Old wood, beautiful painted plates. Black flagstones . . . a tour of the house. A sense of privilege at seeing it . . . Nuff the dog padding silently about. Silence – not even the sea or the wind.' I had no presentiment that just over two years later I would be living there.

At the end of that passage I referred briefly to a matter that had been causing me concern for weeks. A friend had confided in me about something deeply important to her and I felt burdened with the secret, terrified that I would inadvertently reveal it. 'I wish I could talk to George', I wrote, 'but too great a risk.' The next day I rang him to ask if I might call in – though it would certainly not have been to discuss this very private thing – but he seemed preoccupied: 'Speaking to George. Someone there? He did not suggest I go.' I saw him on the following Sunday, however, at the end of a busy day – a friend from Kirkwall to lunch, afternoon coffee with Donella Kirkland at Calum Morrison's, an evening visit to Alison Blacklock. 'And even later than that, I went to see George.' On the following Saturday I went to Mayburn Court to watch Andrei Tarkovsky's final film, *The Sacrifice*, with George; I had seen it before and was happy that George seemed to find it as moving and beautiful as I did. George and I were meeting frequently then; I saw him twice at the end of that week, calling in late at Mayburn Court on my way home from social events.

It was around this time that I was invited to become the literature secretary of the Orkney Arts Society, taking over from my colleague Alistair Peebles. This role primarily involved inviting Scottish writers to come to Orkney to give readings and talks. Although I was pleased when Alistair asked me to take on the job – it was unpaid, of course – I had initially been anxious about my very imperfect knowledge of contemporary Scottish writing. George, however, was encouraging and even rather excited about it, and said that if I took it on he would be glad to advise me. The Scottish Arts Council produced a booklet containing the names and brief biographies of published Scottish writers who were willing to give readings, and George had great fun going through the list with me over several cups of tea: 'Don't, whatever you do, invite him – he'll arrive the worse for drink' (this might have been totally slanderous, but I had no way of knowing), and 'Now he's good, a fine poet. And you'd like her, too. Perhaps you could put her up in your spare room at Faravel.'

I met some remarkable people during my time as literature secretary, and most of them asked to be taken to meet George; many convivial evenings were spent beside the fire at Mayburn Court with glasses of single malt. Margaret Elphinstone was one of those who stayed in my spare room and came with me to visit George, and we kept in touch for a long time afterwards. Jeremy Hilton, one of the first people to give a reading after I had taken over the role from Alistair, came to Stromness on 21 February, and my review in *The Orcadian* (it was always hard to find anyone else willing to do them) explained that the influence of Orkney was powerfully evident in his forthcoming work, *Shadow Engineering*.[11] Other writers who visited Orkney to give readings over the next couple of years included the Canadian writer Robert Bringhurst, George's friend Moira Burgess, Andrew Greig, Alanna Knight, Carl MacDougall and Aileen Paterson.

George had known Moira Burgess for many years; they met at Easter in 1970 when Peter Grant organised a librarians' weekend in Orkney that Moira was eager to attend, having been 'bowled over', she said, by *A Calendar of Love*.[12] John Broom – then living in Caithness – was at that librarians' weekend too. 'We were at the Ayre Hotel in Kirkwall and George came over in the evening', Moira remembered. 'We went to the Easter Vigil in Kirkwall's little Catholic church, full of the symbolism of resurrection and light.'[13] When she returned the following Easter, she had a chance to get to know George better, and in 1985 she brought her children, then aged eleven and six, to Orkney for their first visit. George took a great interest in the children and enjoyed their poems and pictures, which Moira sent to him from time to time. 'I long to see the growth in stature and winsomeness of Kirsten and Peter', he had written to her during the previous autumn. 'It was particularly joyous to see them in the freedom of Rackwick in July '87.'[14] Moira recalled a 'never to be forgotten day' on Hoy when they had been invited over by Peter and Betty Grant: 'George was staying with them at Mucklehouse. It was just about warm enough to sit outside, but there was the hazard of the geese. When they hissed at us, you never saw a poet move so fast to get indoors.'[15]

One Sunday afternoon at the end of February, I was invited with George and other friends to see Sigrid's new home,

Barnhouse, at Birsay. There is no detailed record of this visit in my diary (just 'Sigrid's for tea 2 pm'), but fortunately George wrote about it in 'Under Brinkie's Brae'. Archie and Elizabeth Bevan were there, and so was Marjorie Linklater, and John Broom too, I think, as he seems to be one of the figures in a photograph I took of Sigrid and some of her guests standing outside the house, looking towards the Brough. John didn't get on very well with Marjorie, as I recall, but if there were tensions on that occasion I have forgotten them. 'It happened to be a bright fine day between two storms', George told his readers, and 'already to the north-west, there was an infusion of grey into the blue, and the little white clouds above were teased out and shredding: a sure sign of imminent gale.'[16] He described Birsay as the loveliest of the Mainland parishes, 'steeped in history and perennial beauty', discoursing on a little of that history before returning to the practical details of 'tea and cakes and a small dram'. When George looked through that issue of the *Orcadian*, I wonder if his eye was caught, as mine was, by a sad but delightful article headed 'Oldest Goose Dies' – it was forty-three years old and had lived in Holm, and as far as anybody knew there had never been such a long-lived goose in Orkney. It was the kind of story that George would have enjoyed.

Sunday evening was a time that George and I often spent together; I was at Mayburn Court on the first two Sundays in March, and also on the Friday in between. On the 13th I saw the Northern Lights, the aurora borealis. Alison Blacklock and I met for a drink at the Ferry Inn and came out to find 'a streak of strange light overhead, as if a paintbrush had swept white over the black sky'. As I walked up the Back Road, near the Braes Hotel, the sky was 'extraordinary – frightening even – light streaming from a central corona, so that it seemed as if a second moon was about to emerge from behind the clouds – yet the moon itself shone with an almost unnatural brilliance'. I went home to put on warmer clothes and get a torch before walking through the campsite at Ness Point to stand in the shelter of the wall of the old lifeboat shed and watch the strange shifting lights, with surges of pink and palest green: 'not moving & flickering, as the first time I saw it, but very bright (George said it was seen even in the southern counties)'.

George's name continues to thread through my notes from that month:

14 March. George 9 p.m.

19 March. Yesterday: A heron on the foreshore at Finstown. Summer-blue water. More than thirty swans on the Loch of Stenness. Early evening light: the sea now a deep rich shade; the Orphir hills purple. A walk to Alison's: the sky above Brinkie's Brae a delicate, translucent brightness – no colour at all . . . And *Mishima*[17] with George later . . .

Today: Sunday quiet (only seagulls, & a dog barking), hills & sea soft grey, not much colour, but the sunlight very soft & uncertain & pale . . . The view of sea & hills framed by thick cream curtains, & a large pink stone from Rackwick lying on the white painted sill . . .

After I came back from lunch at the Plout Kirn (with Kirklands & Meeks) I slept in bed for a while, then went to collect George's letters . . . & then went for a walk past Ness . . . I went on a little way, further than I had meant. Hoy very black . . . A single seal. Lights flashing. The wind surging powerfully. Back in the almost-dark. The vernal equinox.

My diary entry for 21 March begins 'To the pub with Gozo.' I went that evening with several friends, including George, to a rather unusual event at the Pier Arts Centre, later described by John Aberdein in a review for *The Orcadian* as 'an evening of haunting brilliance', featuring a young Japanese writer, Gozo Yashimasu. This 'stunning expressive poet' read his poems in Japanese, with the translation 'rendered vigorously by local actor Alex Rigg'. The Orcadian musician Ivan Drever gave an improvised guitar accompaniment to the voices:

> The index of their collective quality as artists was that when they read and played together, none of the audience ... could believe that they had never rehearsed for one minute together. their complementary qualities, occidental and oriental, their harmony, was achieved with that apparent ease only available to the gifted, the disciplined ... Gozo, in evening dress, gold specs and black ribboned hair, read three long poems with strong, amputated gestures, as he traced his symbolism in the air.[18]

My own account was more prosaic and parochial, listing some of my friends and acquaintances who had been amongst the audience:

> I arrived with the Bevans senior ... Alison [Blacklock]. Carol [Dunbar]. George. Phyllis [and] Erlend [Brown] ... John Broom. Beverley looking lovely. Alex. Ivan Drever. At first I found the reading – no, performance – too strange & alienating. But, by the second long poem, was caught up in the flow, the interweaving of voice & voice, word & music, the strange chant-like cadences. Then sushi & Japanese tea.

I wish now that I had noted whether or not George tried the sushi and, if he did, what he thought of it.

On Good Friday I visited Mayburn Court in the evening: 'tea (late) with George and Nora'. I saw George again on Easter Day and he gave me a copy of *A Time to Keep and Other Stories*. My friend Pauline came up from London to stay at Faravel, and her visit meant that although I hadn't yet taken my driving test it was possible to venture out, as long as she was sitting in the passenger seat. My driving skills must have been reasonably good at that stage because on one occasion she fell asleep. I mentioned in a letter to my parents that George came with us on another afternoon, settled safely in the back; he loved to be driven around Orkney, especially in the spring when the daffodils were out, and the blues and greens of sky and grass seemed so vivid after the winter. Pauline wanted to visit Maeshowe, a Neolithic chambered cairn, and George and I went into the nearby café to wait for her:

> Tea at Tormiston Mill with George . . . remember Pam & her mother & the baby . . . Last night: George's. Conversation in a room lit only by firelight. Then the lamp on, & tea, & Renée's cherry cake. I left at nine thirty & walked slowly up the path, my eyes upon the sky, spellbound by the luminosity of the stars.

The baby we admired was Alexandra Ashman, the daughter of Pamela Beasant and Iain Ashman, and George told me, as we sat drinking tea, that he thought Pam a fine poet; we had heard her reading her work at the Foy during the previous winter.

At the beginning of April, a few days after the Tormiston

outing and Pauline's return to London, I spent an evening with George and Brian Murray at the Braes Hotel. The Braes is now a private house, but when I first came to Orkney it was a hotel with a popular bar. It stands at the top of a steep hill and a large window faces out to the hills of Orphir and down Scapa Flow, so it was frustrating to find that the part of the bar with the best view was taken up by the pool table (and, as I subsequently discovered, by the 'Leading Lights' disco on Friday nights), but it was the nearest pub for those of us who lived at the south end and I spent many happy hours there with George, Alison and other friends. It was also the place where George and Brian first met, in the early 1970s. Brian, who was at that time a principal teacher of English (though he later became a headmaster and an educational adviser for Ayrshire), was introduced to George when he was up in Orkney on a school trip, and thus began a long and faithful friendship. 'Tonight: the Braes with GMB & Brian Murray', I wrote. 'George holding my hand in the back of a taxi. I am happy.'

George's presence often had a soothing effect on me, of filling me with contentment and peace – though perhaps on this occasion the amount of alcohol I consumed might also have affected my mood. After his death I remembered that evening and wrote about it in the poem 'Images',[19] although most of the details are lost and only the end remains startlingly clear. It was raining, and Brian arranged for a taxi to take us the short distance down the hill known as Hellihole and along to Mayburn Court in the wet darkness. During the brief drive, George took my hand and held it discreetly, and whispered to me how lucky he felt, 'to have a friend like you'. Later, when I was mourning George, that moment came back vividly into my mind.

I had seen George earlier that day: 'Lord & Lady Temple of Stowe with George & Brian to look round my library . . . George's at eight; Brian comes – the Braes.' The visit to the school had been arranged because Elizabeth Gore-Langton wanted to see the library, which is a fine space – perhaps in some ways the showpiece of the whole building at that time, though the school has expanded since then. It is a large, wood-lined room with a high ceiling, tall windows, and a spiral staircase leading to the study area on the upper floor. I was used to showing visitors around, but not rather grand or titled ones, and I was slightly nervous. All went well, however, and George wrote about the afternoon in 'Under Brinkie's Brae':

> The pupils of the 1980s have spacious and well-stocked apart-ments. Everything conceivable is there to help them cross the border into the enchanted lands of literature, and any other subject they may feel called to. There are computers – which we of the 1930s could never have imagined, any more than we could have imagined people actually walking on the moon . . . We ascended an iron spiral to a quiet study room . . . No library could be more conducive to a true love of books and knowledge.[20]

There are some brief, undated comments in my diary: 'then GMB – Nora ill – watching *Room with a View*'. George was a great admirer of Forster's work, and he enjoyed this film adaptation of the novel, directed by James Ivory. I noted on 8 April that 'I walked to the cemetery & saw the new moon rising over Hoy Sound – back to GMB & a roomful of Webers . . . the too-warm, crowded room.' The Weber family were having a holiday in Orkney but had formerly lived in Stromness at Quildon, the house next door to Renée's cottage, and George was very fond of them. As I recall, he told me that they had a family connection with the Norwegian artist Edvard Munch but I have been unable to confirm this, although Erlend Brown has also heard this story.

George was sometimes described as reclusive, but one would never have thought it on an evening like that – the bright, busy room; the animation and laughter and his obvious pleasure in the company. There were many such occasions when he invited me to Mayburn Court and I arrived to find other guests already there. It may be true that 'an old man withdraws into a narrower circle, just as in November the light lessens',[21] but George's circle, even towards the end, seemed to be full of people, and I have lost count of all those whom I met in his house. They included friends from abroad, one of whom was Karin Meissenburg, who had a family connection to Nora and eventually bought a house in Stromness. Some years later, Karin introduced me to Maryanna Tavener, the wife of the composer Sir John Tavener, who brought her two daughters to our house to play with Emma one afternoon; this was one of the many unexpected encounters that my life in Orkney offered. There were writers – I particularly remember a lovely conversation with the Scottish author Jenny Robertson – and a photographer: Paddy Hughes, with whom George travelled to Ireland in 1968, although I did not know this at the time.

George lamented that I had missed another photographer by an hour or two when Fay Godwin, known primarily for her striking black-and-white landscapes, came to Stromness to call on him during her brief stay at Woodwick House in Evie.

Then there were other friends whom I didn't actually see but who became familiar to me because the telephone would often ring during the evening, especially on a Sunday, and George would chat away, uninhibited by my presence. When I first knew him, I used to disappear tactfully into the kitchen during these conversations, but George soon made it clear that this was unnecessary (and undesirable – I suspect that he preferred not to have his guests fiddling about in his kitchen), so I would sit and read whatever was to hand, trying not to appear unduly interested in what I could hardly help overhearing. That was sometimes quite difficult, as George would be just a few feet away from me, chuckling and exclaiming and recounting the events of the week. When he eventually put down the phone he usually shared much of the news from far away.

He always seemed keen to meet my own visitors, too. During the first few years that I was in Orkney, a stream of friends and relations came to see my new home, and invariably George would urge me to bring them down to Mayburn Court. My parents visited Orkney for the first time in May that year, and when my father wrote to me later that month he added: 'Our kindest regards to Alison, Beverley, Dave and Donella and, in particular, George who made us so welcome.'[22] Beverley was becoming a closer friend: '18 April. Happiness without shadows. Birsay – the beauty and solidity of the ruins of the Earl's Palace ... with Beverley, the light falling on grass and stone ... Scattered farms, peaceful under the sky. I can never leave.'

My life at this time seemed full to the brim with new experiences and friends, and also with a new spiritual intensity. The church had been an intrinsic and important part of my young life, but in my early twenties I experienced a loss of faith and a profound sense of disillusion. At university I read theology as an ancillary subject, and found myself studying the New Testament and learning about the philosophy of religion with an increasing sense of detachment. For more than a decade, from the mid-1970s until the late 1980s, I lived without any clearly defined religious beliefs, but by the time I met George I was searching for a way back and he followed my progress with great interest and patience. Sometimes he asked me to drive him to Kirkwall on a Sunday morning so that he could attend Mass there, and occasionally Brian Murray came too if he was visiting Orkney. On these occasions I usually delivered George to the Catholic church, Our Lady and St Joseph's, before going by myself to St Magnus Cathedral, but once he asked me to attend a special evening Mass with him, and although I could not take a full part in the service I was reassured by the familiarity of the liturgy, remembering phrases that were familiar from childhood, from the Anglican prayer book.

On St Magnus Day, 16 April, I called on George late in the evening, and I saw Nora at Mayburn Court the following week. On the 19th, the Pier Arts Centre hosted a 'Memorable Literary Double Act', consisting of readings by Jane Gardam and Iain Crichton Smith. At the close of the evening, John Broom expressed the audience's appreciation, and I was rather startled when I read the review, which mentioned 'a characteristically feeble vote of thanks by Mr John Broom', until I saw his initials, J.L.B., at the end of the article.[23] On the 22nd I noted '6.30 – Tankerness Museum with George' in my diary, but this is one outing that has been lost in the tangles of memory. But I do remember having lunch with George at Beverley's house, the next day, and John Broom being there as well; we sat at the table beside the window and looked across to Hoy as we ate and talked.

At the beginning of May I set off for Aberdeen on a visit to several schools in the city, hoping to gather ideas for developing the Academy library. I went to see George before I left, and I was able to visit his friends the Grants, in Broomhill Road in Aberdeen, who gave me a splendid Sunday evening dinner. My parents arrived in Orkney just after my return; it was a busy time, and George's name was absent from my diary until I wrote, on 1 June, 'George away.'

The summer of 1989 was an eventful one for George. Much has been made of how little he travelled, but he agreed to go to London and Oxford with Gunnie Moberg as his trusted companion, making fun of his own apprehension: 'A week today and I'll be on my way to Oxford. Who would ever have thought it? It's about as daring as climbing into a space capsule for Mars or the moon!'[24] After an overnight train journey – during which George apparently remained wide awake, as Gunnie later described in the radio programme 'Interrogating Silence' – and a whirlwind tour of London landmarks, they spent a number of pleasant days in Oxford, staying at the home of George's friend and publisher, Hugo Brunner. Writing to my parents on 1 June, I mentioned that 'George is away on the *Ola* today, on his trip to Oxford . . . Last night he sounded in a bit of a panic, but Tam said today that they had got away all right.' As George later mentioned in his column in *The Orcadian*, he and Gunnie planned to break their southbound journey in Pitlochry, staying with Kulgin and Colin (their companions on the Shetland trip), and stop on the way back north for 'a lovely rest among the parks and animals of Druim House at Nairn, where Simon and Sarah [Fraser] live'. On 3 June, George sent a picture postcard of Oxford, telling me his news and letting me know that he would be thinking of me when I took my driving test later that week:

> Hugo Brunner met Gunnie & me at Euston . . . we saw a few London places before Oxford. So much has happened in 2½ days! We had a pleasant time with our friends at Loch Tummel. Here in Oxford are 5 beautiful children and 2 cats rather like Billie, tho' one is elderly and the other very young. This afternoon I saw graduates voting for the Professor of Poetry: everybody thinks Seamus Heaney will get it. I met the retiring incumbent, Peter Levi . . . I have just come in from sitting for an hour in the sun in the lovely garden. On Tuesday 2 separate BBC radio folk are coming to see me – an ordeal . . . I do hope you're well, Jo, and that soon you'll have the freedom of the roads. We might be home next Saturday. Gunnie has gone maybe for a shopping splurge.[25]

The Telegraph Weekend Magazine published an account of his trip, full of striking detail. Describing London, George wrote:

> There was blue sky overarching the city, laced with high thick white cloud. I was aware of a complexity-within-unity. But minute by minute the traffic was thickening, and the isolated early morning stirrers were becoming groups and crowds hastening hither and thither. The 'mighty heart' that Wordsworth saw from Westminster Bridge does not 'lie still' for long in the late 1980s.

In Oxford he had seen that 'the "brickish skirt" that Gerard Manley Hopkins found so disfiguring in the 1860s has mellowed with time. There are streets of gracious brick-built honey-coloured houses all about "the dreaming spires"; in one of them we stayed, amid much comfort and kindness.'[26]

In spite of enjoying the delights of Oxford, both Gunnie and George wanted to be back in Orkney in time for the St Magnus Festival. On the journey home they stayed, as planned, with Simon and Sarah Fraser, and George wrote lyrically about the visit in 'Under Brinkie's Brae': 'At Inverness, Simon was waiting to drive us to the lovely house in Nairn, in an enchanted enclosure of tall trees, blossoms, Arab horses, big gentle dogs, and an exquisite cat called Sireadh, "the seeker" in Gaelic.'[27]

Nora, usually stranded in Deerness by a scarcity of buses and her difficulties in learning to drive, came to stay with me at Faravel for the festival, as George's spare room was already promised to other visitors, and we went to a few of the events together. A highlight of the festival for me was seeing a performance by the percussionist Evelyn Glennie. On 17 June, Claire Nielson and Paul Greenwood, whom I met at Mayburn Court, presented *The Realms of Gold*, an anthology and commentary created for the festival by George. The title was taken from a line written by Keats, to indicate, George said, 'that this personal anthology is a kind of voyage, from the first intoxicating discovery in youth . . . and somewhere along the way you sign on gladly, and for life'. At the festival performance, readings of the poems were interspersed with George's commentary, although it was Archie Bevan, rather than George, who gave the readings, since George disliked public appearances of that kind. His text conveyed the wonder and the importance of poetry and gave his own responses to great works, referring to Sir Patrick Spens, Shelley, Milton, Yeats, Ecclesiastes, Hardy, Dylan Thomas and others:

'What is the secret of the realms of gold? Why should words in certain patterns give us such delight? Behind the words, behind the meanings and images, there was a deeper mystery . . . every island in the realms of gold has, somewhere, its hidden temple, and there, in the precincts, is an ancient spring, a sacred well, guarded by four veiled figures: Time and Chance and Fate and Mortality. They have been there from the beginning, guarding the waters; they will be there to the end . . .

It may be, all our lives after infancy is a flight from reality, from those inescapable things, Time and Fate and Chance and Mortality . . . they will overshadow us in the end.

George went on to explain his view of the true purpose of poetry: 'to enable us to come to terms with those powers that cannot be denied, that surround us wherever we turn'. Poetry, he believed, has the power to reconstruct the way in which we see and experience the world: 'the Furies . . . are transfigured, they become the kindly ones; the powers we have feared have been our friends always. But this knowledge doesn't come easily or soon.'

Another of the festival events was the first screening of *Venus Peter* (filmed in Orkney the previous year) at the old Phoenix cinema in Kirkwall – it was shown again for several days in November 1989. The film was based on the book by Christopher Rush, *A Twelvemonth and a Day*,[28] which I was pleased to find in the school library, and Moira Burgess recently sent me an article that Rush wrote about George in 2004, in which he mentioned meeting him and sharing a meal with him. I am indebted to Moira for introducing me to a very funny story told by Rush, dating from George's Newbattle Abbey days, which involved a group of friends trying to get an inebriated and resistant George, who was hanging on for dear life to a radiator pipe, into his room. Rush had found this story hard to reconcile – as indeed did I – with the gentle, rather fragile appearance of the man he later met.[29]

When I visited George on 26 June he seemed happy to be at home again, sitting quietly in the familiar surroundings of Mayburn Court after all the unaccustomed excitement of his visit to England and the bustle of the St Magnus Festival. His room looked especially lovely that evening:

Then at George's . . . A rainbow across Stenness, a high, almost perfect arc (& a second bow shimmering palely behind it), confirming my sense of peace . . . pretty flowers, from Nora's Deerness garden, in a vase on the table – poppies, delphiniums, white & yellow blossom too – & a glass of Laphroaig, & still the sense of perfect peace, of being lulled. Whereas earlier . . . a sense of unease – & exhausted.

As this suggests, in spite of my buoyant happiness in the spring, the summer was a time of fluctuating emotions. One great pleasure, however, had been the promised exhibition at the Pier Arts Centre in June and early July of pictures by Sir Sidney Nolan. As well as the private view on a Friday evening, 9 June, there was also a question-and-answer session on Saturday afternoon. John Broom introduced me to the artist and Lady

Nolan; according to a letter to my parents, 'we had quite a chat. I first saw some of Nolan's work when I was in Southampton – and never could have dreamt that I'd ever meet the man.' I went back again and again to look at the paintings, and the poster for the exhibition still hangs on my living-room wall.

Early in July, George had to suffer one of the things he dreaded most – being interviewed for a television programme by a team from Glasgow – but he survived unscathed.[30] On the 10th, I wrote: 'Saturday . . . the calm happiness of the morning . . . Afterwards, at the Pierhead, we met George & Brian Murray, sitting on a seat, Brian with a suitcase of washing.' George probably already knew that he would have to pack his own suitcase soon for a visit to Aberdeen Royal Infirmary, and I eventually heard about this, mentioning in a letter to my parents that I was anxious about him. I had dinner with Dorrie and Donald Morrison one evening later that month and then went on to Mayburn Court: 'At nine I left to visit George (having telephoned first) – the Grants & Paddy [Hughes] there, so after a small whisky I went home . . . happy & safe – anxious only for George, but Betty is comfortable [i.e. comforting] and reassuring.'

George had been so reticent about his illness that I failed to realise just how worried I should be. John Broom must have been extremely concerned, for he did something that seemed extraordinarily out of character to anyone who knew him well. He had a strong antipathy to the Orkney Christian Fellowship and disapproved of the fact that I had begun to go along sometimes to their Sunday services (held in the dining hall at the Academy) with Calum Morrison, but in my diary I mentioned 'some news (which Calum gave me early as we drank coffee). John Broom had stopped Calum in the street & asked him to go & pray with? for? George . . . My heart goes out to that strange, dark man for this . . . John had asked if he [Calum] had a moment to spare [and] seemed urgent in his manner, agitated.' Earlier in the year, John, who was a Unitarian, had caused a stir on the letters page of *The Orcadian* by expressing some of his views about religion, and a number of people had written in to take issue with him, one of whom regretted that 'Mr John Broom, in his recent letter regards the Christian doctrine of salvation through repentance of faith as "immoral" '.[31]

George and John had recently had one of their occasional clashes. Earlier that month, on 13 July, I had been at Kirkwall airport to meet my friend Sue from London – she was one of the many visitors who came with me to Mayburn Court for an evening, and I remember George asking her with great interest about the choir in which she sang. Waiting for the plane to land, I saw the Morrison family and went across to talk to them. Someone had bought a copy of *The Orcadian* and I noted afterwards that 'we all read George's article ticking off John Broom', although in fact this misrepresents George's words. This was his opening sentence: 'John L. Broom and I don't always see eye to eye on matters of religion and literature, but we never fall out seriously with each other.'[32] I was aware that George and John had known each other for a long time, but it was only when I read Maggie Fergusson's biography that both the extent and the limitations of their friendship became clear to me.[33] They had been contemporaries in Edinburgh and there had been rivalry between them – Fergusson mentions that Stella Cartwright had to fend off John's apparently unwanted attentions.[34]

I spent several evenings with George over the next couple of weeks before he set off for Aberdeen on 31 July, laden with the hopes and prayers of his friends. Soon afterwards, I travelled down on the overnight ferry, the MV *St Sunniva*, to visit him – not in the hospital, but in the far more congenial setting of the Grants' home in Broomhill Road, since George was allowed out of hospital at weekends. He loved being with Peter and Betty and their son Alan, and we had a meal together at their house, where a large Sylvia Wishart painting hung on the dining-room wall. Afterwards, I was never quite able to recall that painting clearly – what remained was simply an impression of beauty and rich colour – but I was happy to think that I recognised it amongst several works owned by Betty Grant that were included in the exhibition of Sylvia's work at the Pier Arts Centre in 2011.[35] As we sat talking after dinner it was immensely reassuring to find George cheerful – or at least maintaining an appearance of cheerfulness.

Back in Ward 6 at the infirmary he must have spent many hours writing letters, for he was a faithful correspondent and I know that he kept in touch with dozens of friends and relatives. In Stromness, George and I saw each other so often that there had never been any need to write to each other, and thus the letter I received at this time was the first I had ever had from him, apart from the postcard he sent from Oxford. He wrote:

It was lovely of you to come and see me on Sunday evening. That was altogether a happy/busy day.

I'd rather be in Rackwick or Birsay than here, especially after the sun broke through this afternoon.

It's a strange existence, lounging in bed and eating rather starchy meals in a too warm ward, and occasionally being bounced on [perhaps he meant 'pounced'?] and led away down long corridor for an X-ray or some other test. I'm having some trouble trying to damp down the transistors that are such a menace here. I brought the 2 Tchehov volumes my tipsy literature-loving friend brought me as an apology for bursting in on me on Saturday night . . . I'm finding the stories fascinating

They're all very kind here but I feel like someone bewildered in a strange world.[36]

And a few days later:

Many thanks for your phone call and letter. They did cheer me. Now I have a phone card and once I've learned the technique I may phone you . . .

They've started giving me a course of X-ray therapy, to last 25 sessions (5 sessions a week). Not distressing so far, but the preliminary scans were trying a bit. The staff are very pleasant. The food quite good. Not a harsh regime at all.

I'll only be back at the beginning of autumn. But I do look forward to see you in mid-August . . . Today the big windows are blind with fog . . .

I think the Grants may be in Rackwick. I'll feel more at home when they return.

With love, dear Jo. Enjoy the second half of summer.[37]

George did partly master the technique of phone cards, but on at least one occasion his credit ran out and we were cut off in mid-flow. I was spending some time in London that month, seeing family and friends, and had hoped that on the way back north I would be able to break my journey to visit George again, but train and boat connections made it difficult, and the cattery where I had left Billie was unable to keep her for an extra couple of days. In his next letter, George wrote:

I tried twice to phone you in London but both times I couldn't get through.

Probably in Aberdeen tomorrow (Sat.). You'll phone the hospital and find the bird has fled . . . I'm staying the weekend at the Grants'. Peter fetched me before lunch and I enjoyed a nice pizza (with tuna) cooked by Alan . . .

I'm quite happy at the hospital – the NHS is a wonderful set-up – but the treatment, though it shows signs of working already, makes one tired and short-tempered a bit. Doctors and nurses are wonderful.

I'd have been happy, Jo, to have had your company, however briefly, in hospital. Now I must wait, it seems, until you get home and rescue Billie . . .

(Now it's poor Gypsy's turn for incarceration: I think Nora may be on her way south. She'll stop at Nairn and stay a day or two with Simon and Sarah Fraser before going on to Edinburgh . . . I could have been this weekend at Nairn too, but thought it just too far away, with the side effects of radiotherapy, etc.)

I do hope you had a good time, dear Jo, and met old friends and visited well-loved places.

I have been swamped by mail and visitors. Never will all letters get answered! I try to write 2 or 3 a day, and my mini 'Orcadian' article, and letter to Gypsy of course; and I've even tried to write some verse that didn't come off quite.

Much love.[38]

I wanted to keep in touch with him, of course, and he declared in 'Under Brinkie's Brae' that letters from Orkney when he was in hospital were 'like draughts of fresh air'[39]. At the same time I felt guilty for having burdened him with correspondence, because he seemed to feel duty-bound to write back immediately, referring once to 'a deluge of mail'.[40] My summer had been busy, as a stream of friends – from London, Brighton, Glasgow and even the Seychelles – had been staying at Faravel, but nevertheless I felt strangely isolated in George's absence. Alison and Beverley were also away for a while, and I noted a conversation with Calum: 'What came out was . . . my need of Alison and George. And confessed my loneliness . . . after all these weeks of needing space, I get it and fall apart.'

I commented in a letter to my parents on 21 August that George had just telephoned, sounding cheerful. He said he'd been pleased to have a letter and a photograph from them: during their stay in Orkney in May, George had come with us on an outing to Birsay and we took some pictures. My parents sent him a copy of one to remind him of that cheerful day, but although he is smiling I'm struck now by how fragile he appears, against the backdrop of the Earl's Palace.

In September, much to everyone's relief, George returned to Stromness. He mentioned in 'Under Brinkie's Brae' that his stay in Aberdeen had 'gone on for five and a half weeks'.[41] It might have been just before his return to Mayburn Court that he went to Kirkwall to stay with his sister-in-law, Hazel (his brother Norrie's widow), for a short period to recuperate before going to his own house. I visited him there, and I remember Hazel's kindness to me and her concern for George, but the date is lost and this was perhaps at the end of another hospital stay. I noted, however, that we had 'Drinks with the Countess' at Garth on 5 September and I saw George twice during the following week, once at Mayburn Court and again when he came for a meal at Faravel with Beverley and Calum. After all he had been through in Aberdeen he must have been exhausted, yet he not only remembered my birthday and gave me *Andrina and Other Stories*, but also found the time to write yet another acrostic:

Just when we think, autumn lies
Over the shorn fields
And in purple upon the hills, and snow is weaving on
    stark looms
North beyond Cape Farewell and Spitzbergen,
Now we remember too
All good things by autumn given:

Red in fires and apples – a new coat for Billie –
A first Aurora, heavy swirling silks –
Marmalade and beetroot, a summer hoard, in the
    cupboard –
Summonses by friends for wine laughter music –
Enthrongment of stars over Orphir – Today
Your birthday, Joanna, in September.

We slipped back into our old routines for a while and created new ones too, for I had passed my driving test at the first attempt and it was now possible for me to take George out without someone else accompanying us. On Saturday or Sunday afternoons, if George had no other engagements, a favourite destination was Warebeth beach. I would park the car there and we would walk towards the ruins of Breckness House along the coast – although we never got that far – with George insisting that we 'cross the burn for luck'. We went unhurriedly, enjoying the view of Hoy and sometimes, on a clear day, of the Sutherland hills, and he told me many stories: about life in Orkney during the Second World War; about filling sandbags at the edge of the old golf course; about traces of gold being found in a burn up at Yesnaby. These were happy times; in spite of the long spells in hospital and his apparent frailty he seemed content for a while, and I was glad to have his company.

At the beginning of October I was busy planning a reading by Carl MacDougall:

> The weather was grey, slightly chilled, an atmosphere of negativity ... exhausted, knowing I <u>had</u> to ring Carl MacDougall, <u>must</u> see George – So all this happened – but with what unexpected ease and pleasure. Carl had been trying to ring me ... we arranged a tentative date for his reading. Then I went to George's – to find a man from the National Library of Scotland bundling up George's correspondence into plastic bags & cardboard files – for the manuscript archives. We had much good talk about poets & letters, & he got out all George's small-press limited editions to look at them ... And I will write later about Sunday afternoon – George calling.

I never did write about that afternoon, and the memory is lost.

George's life was still shadowed by illness, and this meant having to travel back and forth between Orkney and the mainland for treatment that could not be provided at the Balfour

Hospital in Kirkwall. He made no fuss about it. On 12 October he wrote to Moira Burgess, telling her that he had missed being in Rackwick that summer – 'that was a sore deprivation' – because he been in hospital in Aberdeen, but he did not add that he was about to set off again: 'Nothing much happens here, which suits me just fine. I get on with my work in the mornings. My latest work doesn't seem to be so gladly received as the writings of 15–20 years ago. Ah well, I'm not complaining. I'll keep doing it as long as I enjoy it.' He also gave Moira a rather startling piece of news about John Broom, who 'left this afternoon for Aberdeen, Blantyre and *Albania* (of all places!)'. George expressed his pleasure in knowing that Moira would be in Orkney again in the spring, as I had invited her to give a reading: 'I'm glad you're coming to read in Stromness in the spring. You'll find Joanna Ramsey very pleasant to deal with. And the Pier Arts Centre is a good place for readings and music as well as for art . . . A novel by you is always an exciting event. I lent your last book to Joanna' (this was *A Rumour of Strangers*, published in 1987).

Later that month I spent the evening with George and Renée, watching a Truffaut film, *Le Dernier Métro*, on television, remarking later that 'Renée [was] friendlier than I have known her, remembering Paris which she left in 1923 (when she was 23 herself).' The next day, I saw George from my window as he walked slowly past Faravel to have lunch with Renée, and he called in to see me on his way back. I must have been reassured by his stoicism and his calm acceptance of his illness, because although I knew he was about to return to Aberdeen for treatment – he left Orkney on 23 October – I somehow sensed that all would be well:

An unexpected feeling of tremendous joy and relief and well-being . . . I delivered George's letters – had a quiet, tidying-up day . . . Then I drove to the airport – picked up three KGS [Kirkwall Grammar School] lasses in Finstown who were full of giggles at the success of their first-ever attempt at hitching. When I said I was going to see off GMB, they wanted to come & get his autograph, but in case they were serious about it, I dissuaded them.

I thought that George would be feeling anxious and not up to dealing with young fans, but perhaps I was wrong to be so protective – he might have enjoyed the distraction. I dropped off the girls and went on to the airport:

Got there early, safely, & G. & the Bevans arrived soon after – sat for a few minutes having coffee before his flight [was] called. Then I grasped his hand & he kissed me goodbye & went . . . I watched the plane take off & then drove back – dark cloud and rather livid gleams of sun. Near Tormiston, a deluge – could see nothing but water pouring over the windscreen . . . Stromness strangely lit, with blue brightness looming up behind Hoy, the intense darkness of the rainclouds breaking apart . . . so overwhelmed by this extraordinary feeling of peace that it was necessary to write it down.

I wanted both the sense of peace and the dramatic sky to be good omens for George, and was happy when he wrote comfortingly and kindly on 26 October:

It was lovely talking to you on the phone just now. I'm having strange experiences with that card-phone. Yesterday, twice trying to get Stromness numbers, I was answered by a rather refined Aberdeen lady. 'Are you sure you've got the right code?' says she the second time . . . Dr Hurman is pleased with my health but has advised 6 more 'shots' of radiotherapy. Tomorrow I'll have shot 3, so we're halfway there.

Yesterday, to while away the time after breakfast, I started work on a Christmas story and it seems to be OK so far. The end will be the difficult part. Good fun, as always.

Thank goodness my 2 ward-mates don't like TV much. They don't like books either. I dunno exactly how they pass their days . . .

Tomorrow I'll go to spend the weekend at the Grants' – the best hotel in Aberdeen.

The book of Faroese short stories that Gunnie gave me is wonderful. William Heinesen is still alive at 90: a great writer. You must read him, Jo.

How's Billie now the cold dark nights are here?

I'm looking forward very much to see you again, dear Jo. Round about Thursday, I think, is the date . . . But I'll phone you before then.[42]

Early in November I was able to tell my parents that 'George is out of hospital, staying with his friends in Aberdeen, coming home tomorrow.' And he was well enough to come to dinner at Faravel twice in one week: on the 6th with Dorrie and Donald, and again on the 10th: 'G & C here', I noted. The second initial referred to Carl MacDougall, who had arrived in Orkney to give his reading at the Pier Arts Centre, and I fetched him from the airport in my car, taking George with me. Unless the visiting writers were staying at Faravel, I usually booked a room for them with Gloria and John Wallington, who offered bed & breakfast at their home in Alfred Street, close to Mayburn Court. George called there to collect Carl and they walked up to Faravel together to have a meal before the reading. Carl emailed me recently about this: 'I later found out that George hardly ever went to readings and I remember glancing up to see his head at different angles.'[43] It was a memorable and at times hilarious evening, as I described in the review:

> The proceedings opened with a brief masterpiece of wit . . . a prose piece which already threatens to become legendary, and to which no review could do justice . . . If we wondered (some of us wiping tears of mirth from our eyes) whether the rest of the evening could possibly live up to this, we quickly found that it could.[44]

I went on to mention some of the stories from Carl's collection *Elvis Is Dead*[45] and he also read an extract from his novel *Stone Over Water*.[46] At the end of the evening, John Aberdein summed up everyone's appreciation and enjoyment in a vote of thanks, and the review finished with a note of gratitude to Erlend Brown and Maureen Gray for their help – Maureen, now retired, was a stalwart member of staff at the Pier Arts Centre, who worked tirelessly to make sure that things ran smoothly. After the reading, Carl was invited to a housewarming party, but George and I didn't go along – George would have wanted to be getting home to his bed. But Carl recalls spending a lovely afternoon with George, and on Saturday I took Carl out in the car to show him the Ring of Brodgar and other sights, and we had a long conversation about faith and the meaning of life. This visit was the only time that Carl met George, although they had been in contact before the reading and were in touch many times afterwards; George often wrote to Carl, inviting him back, but it wasn't possible for him to come until years later, after George's death. 'I've been in Orkney many times since', Carl wrote in an email to me, 'but nothing has quite matched that first visit with you and George coming into Kirkwall to meet me, George's cheery wave and the trip to Stromness. I remember coming to the top of the hill and looking down on the town.' The MV *St Ola* – now replaced by the MV *Hamnavoe* – was in the harbour. ' "Look, Carl", said George, "the boat's all lit up." '[47]

At the start of the following week, I was walking home quite late after visiting friends, and as I went along Alfred Street the shining flagstones seemed to be shifting and undulating. It took a few moments to realise that a number of large crabs had somehow escaped from premises nearby and were lumbering across the road. Someone else came along and we attempted to gather up the crabs and put them in a safe place, but they could move with such surprising speed that it was a bit like trying to herd cats, and after a while I was helpless with laughter. This was just the kind of tale that George enjoyed and I would certainly have recounted the incident to him when we met: 'Sunday drive with George – Warebeth – Yesnaby – Skaill – Brodgar by moonlight.' I added that 'we went up past Brodgar just as the moon was coming up', and a week or so afterwards I found our outing described with far greater eloquence in 'Under Brinkie's Brae':

'At Warebeth, on a recent Sunday afternoon, the late sun was just clearing the Kame of Hoy in its descent . . .

The clouds over the north coast of Scotland scattered suddenly and we saw the mountains of Sutherland clear-etched, like the serrated teeth of a saw . . .

At Yesnaby, twenty minutes or so later, a frail wan disc lingered at the edge of a cloud. It was the moon, a few days from the full.

'Art thou pale for weariness?' the poet Shelley questioned the moon, when the moon must have looked just like that late November afternoon, a worn washed seashell.

But as we drove home from Skaill, later, by way of Brodgar, the moon came into her own. The brilliance increased, until the full orb was the most beautiful thing in the universe . . .

Quickly the twilight thickened. More and more brilliant, the moon went softly up the sky. When the car came over the Cairston ridge, there lay Stromness with its maze of lights.[48]

Earlier in the year we had taken a similar route, going round by the Bay of Skaill and back past the Ring of Brodgar. On that occasion, an oystercatcher was too slow to rise from the tarmac and I was unable to avoid hitting it. There was a horrible thud, and a drift of plumage fell around the car.

'Oh George!' I remember crying in anguish, 'I've killed it!'

'Oh no, Jo', he said comfortingly, 'I'm sure it will be all right.' Alas, in the rear-view mirror I could see a sad mess of black and white feathers in the road, but I didn't have the heart to tell him.

The end of the year was a turbulent time. There were some memorable moments – 'opening of Christmas exhibition . . .

The Northern Lights were in the sky, glimmering . . . An arc of light but no movement' – but the black dog sat on my shoulder. I was doing battle again with the depression and anxiety that have recurred for periods throughout my life, although I have been more or less free of them for the past few years. This inner darkness was something that George and I had in common, although it was a long time before I realised it because he was so good at hiding his suffering. I found his presence comforting when I was in a low mood because he never minded if we didn't talk much, and it was possible to sit in companionable silence.

Another person I saw often at this time was Dorrie Morrison's mother, Alice Agate, who was in her nineties and lived in sheltered housing at Rae's Close; most people knew her as 'Lal' but she insisted that I should call her 'Granny', the Morrisons having become a sort of second family to me. Sometimes we watched *Coronation Street* and during the adverts she made tea and gave me a slice of 'Granny's pink', her home-made cake; she seemed to like me being there and I always felt safe and comfortable at Rae's Close, just as I did at Mayburn Court. Thus, on 'Sunday December 3rd . . . I rang Granny. And later went to George's and came home happier.' Earlier that day I had called at Dorrie and Donald's: 'I went to the Morrisons early & walked Mayling [their dog] to the shore. It was grey & misty & wet but I was not unhappy. Great love for the farms & the burn & water rushing through the ditches, & the low white sky. Wet cows standing patiently.' But later that evening I was feeling 'utterly alone' and by Tuesday my 'tiredness & depression' were 'almost overwhelming'.

I saw George again at the end of that week, on a busy Saturday – I had coffee with my friend Chris Meek and then went home

to 'dig garden & tidy lupins & lift last potatoes'. Beverley came
to tea '& after G. rang we went for an hour – Nora there. Not
so friendly these days. There is a darkness in her – I remember
the dream she told me – witches.' I didn't know that Nora
was seriously ill again and didn't understand until later that
she must have been desperately worried about her future. Like
George, she did not make a great fuss about illness, even when
it was life-threatening – Geoffrey Elborn's obituary mentions
her 'uncomplaining courage which was humbling'.[49] As well as
being anxious about Nora, George was troubled about another
matter during November; he was sure that there were rats in his
house, having heard faint sounds of scrabbling and gnawing,
and the idea preyed on his mind – he wrote briefly about it in
'Under Brinkie's Brae', mentioning his 'small shiver of fear' at
the thought of them: 'a bead of sweat came on my forehead.
The imagination feeds unwholesomely on such a small sinister
hint.'[50]

    In the midst of these more serious worries, I was also fretting
about having to organise the annual Christmas Foy (which
later became a New Year Foy), as this was one of my duties as
literature secretary. It was intended to be a celebration of local
writing, although I realised that there was no point in trying
to persuade George to give a reading – I had been warned that
such public performances were anathema to him. But he readily
agreed to come along and to write a review for *The Orcadian*,
and I found five poets who were willing to take part. Bessie
Skea, or Grieve, was a friend of George's, and as well as writing
poetry she contributed a regular column ('A Countrywoman's
Diary') to *The Orcadian*. George and I visited her together at
her house in Harray on 18 November, and a photograph taken

by Bessie shows George and me sitting next to one another, looking rather bashful. George is wearing a blue polo-necked shirt under one of his mustard-coloured pullovers (probably knitted for him by Surinder's friend Mrs Moyle) and a brown corduroy jacket. Bessie's house was a short distance along the Dounby road after the turn-off from the main Stromness to Kirkwall road, where the wind whips across the land; it was a wild afternoon and as we struggled to get out of the car I feared that George would be blown away. But the house was cosy and Bessie gave us a warm welcome; we drank tea and ate cake and conversed merrily as it grew darker and stormier outside. As I recall, Bessie had recently been to Australia, or was about to go there, and we found some common ground because one of my sisters, Judy Campbell, lives in Perth in Western Australia. We eventually got round to discussing the reading and Bessie seemed pleased to be taking part.

The Foy was arranged for 12 December and it went well, in spite of impending bad weather. After Beverley had helped me to load all the food and drink into my car (I had made a giant Dundee cake, amongst other things), we decided that the road surface was too icy to risk driving, and repacked everything into baskets which we lugged along the slippery street. The musicians arrived, I noted, 'in a flurry of snow'. I had worried about Bessie getting in from Harray on roads that might be treacherous, but she arrived safely, as did the other performers: Fiona MacInnes, one of the daughters of George's friends Ian and Jean MacInnes; Edward (Eddie) Cummins, to whom George had given encouragement; Pam Beasant, whose work I had heard George praise; and John Aberdein, who taught English at the Academy and is now a well-regarded writer. George's review describes John's

contribution as 'a series of sombre strong meditations on war
. . . balanced by a long monologue in Scots on an incident from
Moby Dick'; Bessie's offering was 'sensitive nature poems and
reminiscence of a vanished Orkney'; and Pam's was 'a sequence
of very moving poems on her experience of childbirth' and 'a
monologue, from Salieri, Mozart's contemporary'. Edward
Cummins was 'a new and highly promising talent . . . his verse
is full of stars, oceans, tides, salt . . . beautifully crafted'; and
Fiona MacInnes was praised for her 'exquisite eye for nature, as
we might expect from a poet who is an artist too . . . She has,
too, a deep sympathy, memorably expressed, for the unfortu-
nates of the earth . . . [and] a gift for biting satire . . . And she
delivers it straight from the shoulder.'[51]

It was a great relief to me that Eddie Cummins had actually
turned up to read at the Foy. He was a fine poet, whose work
George admired and endorsed, and a larger-than-life character,
tall and imposing, with wild dark hair. Eddie died tragically,
far too young, and a book of his poems, *I Flame at Words*, was
published posthumously. I read some of his work before we met,
and wrote to him (he lived at Quarrel Braes in Evie) to say that
I would enjoy talking to him about it. 'I had no fears entrusting
my poems to your care', he replied. 'Please do look forward to
discussing my work with me. You could tell me about your
work. George and I don't say over much, really. So please do
not feel inarticulate. I have great difficulty expressing myself.'
Yet I always felt slightly intimidated by Eddie, and when I
caught sight of him once in a Kirkwall supermarket I began
to creep along the next aisle with my head down, only to hear
Eddie's voice booming out: 'Are you trying to hide from me,
Joanna?' He was a merchant seaman, and before the Foy there

was no word from him for a while: on 5 December I noted that 'Eddie has really gone south. I dread the reading next Tuesday', although George had faith in him and tried to reassure me. On the 9th I was at Dorrie and Donald's for the evening, and just after I arrived 'there was a phone call – for me! Or rather for Donald, but a man trying to find me. Jeremy . . . A friend of Eddie's. Eddie *is* coming back. But a slight mystery as to who this Jeremy is or why he rang Donald when he wanted me.' And the next day, when I called on the Morrisons again, their eldest son was there with his children, 'and the mysterious Jeremy had called *him* yesterday, to ask for my number. Stranger & stranger!' The gist of both calls, however, was that I was not to worry, it would be all right on the night and Eddie would be there. I rushed home 'in heavy rain – to leave a note for John Broom . . . rang George'. On 11 December I had been tired and grumpy, and when George rang me to ask if Eddie had been in touch I was rather abrupt.

Afterwards, I was remorseful: 'I know I was a wee bit short with him. But he seems insistent just now . . . I feel suffocated.' The Foy was only two days away and I was feeling under pressure, wanting it to be a success. I was so relieved when people seemed to enjoy it that 'at the end I felt as high as a kite, loving everybody'. Yet I was concerned about George, because he seemed slightly dependent on me just then and I was mindful that I would be away from Orkney during the Christmas holiday. With hindsight, I see how utterly tactless it was of me to ring one of George's older friends about this, gently suggesting that George might be glad of some more company. I didn't get quite the response I had anticipated. It seemed that some of those who had known and cared about George for many years were growing weary of Renée's proprietorial attitude, and were hurt, I sensed (though it was not tacitly admitted), that she was often given precedence. There was an underlying implication that George shouldn't have let this happen, and having made his bed he must lie on it. I felt slightly shaken afterwards and worried that I had made matters worse.

The snowy weather continued: '14 December . . . a pale cold sky with deep grey snow clouds massed up around the Orphir Hills. Snow on Hoy & everywhere. The water a silky sheet, almost perfectly still.' On the 20th I described a peaceful, pleasant evening beside George's fire with Mary Moore, and I was delighted when George gave me *The Masked Fisherman and Other Stories* for my Christmas gift. But by the next day my mood was much lower, and on the 22nd, before I boarded the afternoon plane to London, I wrote of a sense of 'deep loneliness and impending despair as I walked up the darkening street . . . I can't remember later, perhaps I went to George's . . . The wind, which now I remember had kept me awake much of the night, was tearing wildly from the east, the sea was high, lots of fishing boats in, taking shelter.'

I was spending Christmas with my parents and arrived at their house in reasonable spirits, but on Boxing Day I recorded my depression and panic. I seemed to feel that people wanted too much from me – 'Just say No', I wrote – and George's name was included in a brief list of others whose claims I felt I must resist for a while. 'Tired, irritable, guilty', I added later, although there were some happier days too, and I was glad to meet up with Tim Morrison, Dorrie and Donald's youngest son, who was living in London at the time, and we walked in Holland Park in a grey mist. When I went out to dinner one evening I wore the turquoise and silver necklace that Nora made, which was much admired, and everyone wanted to hear about my life in Orkney.

Amongst other worries at this time, I was anxious about seeing John Broom again. My early encounters with John were often in the Stromness bookshop (its official name is Stromness Books & Prints but it still has, at the time of writing, the faded legend 'J. L. Broom, Bookseller' above the door) and he was always friendly and kind in those days, giving me advice about ordering books for the school and generally being helpful. As the months passed, however, he began to make pointed remarks about my visits to Mayburn Court and was increasingly scornful about my involvement with the Christian Fellowship. He knew that I spent many evenings with George and appeared to find it hard to understand my reluctance to visit him at his own house in Franklin Road, but the reason for this was that I never felt at ease with John in the way that I did with George.

John was an interesting and essentially good-hearted man but, even before he had a stroke that caused his behaviour to become quite uninhibited, his conversation tended to be loaded with humorous innuendo that made me more uncomfortable than he realised. I had noticed that when George talked to me about John it was in an affectionate but frequently exasperated way, and he sympathised with my discomfort about John's manner towards me, which often amounted to an odd kind of flirtatiousness that John probably thought I enjoyed. On several occasions John teased me about marriage and once, half-jokingly, he proposed to me. Instead of being flattered or amused, I felt embarrassed. He was much older than me and we had very little in common, yet there appeared to be an undertone of serious intent in his words and I didn't know how to respond. Two years later, when he heard that I was to marry again, he came up to me in the street and exclaimed loudly, to the bemusement of several passers-by, 'You faithless wench! You were supposed to marry me!'

Towards the end of the year, Sigrid invited me to lunch and asked if I would give a lift to John, who was to be one of the other guests. I had qualms about the kind of conversation that John and I might have on the drive to Birsay in the winter darkness, and instead of sensibly making a polite excuse I not only confessed to Sigrid that I would really prefer not to go if John would be there, but also confided my dilemma to one or two friends. Somehow this found its way back to John. He had already worked himself up into a state of rage about the Christian Fellowship, and my thoughtless and perhaps cruel rejection of his company seemed to take his anger to another level. On 19 December he came to Faravel, late in the evening, and pushed a thick envelope through the letterbox. It contained thirteen pages of closely written script that combined a diatribe against evangelical Christianity with personal criticism of me. It upset me deeply, and although I immediately destroyed the letter it was a long time before the impact of his words faded. George and I discussed this incident and I sometimes wished I had kept the letter to show him, but that would probably have been unfair to both John and George. From a position of neutrality, George was able to continue his friendship with both of us.

In spite of this anxiety about John, the sight of Orkney, after I had been in London for a week, seemed to lift my mood for a while: 'I was happy as we flew over the South Isles . . . Joyfully

I drove to collect Billie, delighting in the hills and colours and water – glad, glad, glad to be back.' And I added later: 'how can I leave here? A faint dust of snow on Hoy hills as I walked up the Back Road to Springfield . . . This seems to be where I belong. Or would other hills, other beaches, do instead?' This suggests that in spite of Orkney's delights, and the fact that I was beginning to think about buying a house instead of renting, I felt restless: a trip to the mainland often unsettled me (and sometimes still does). When I visited friends and familiar places in England there was a sense of detachment or estrangement; I was not quite the same person that I had been before.

I went to a service in St Magnus Cathedral but noted that 'George didn't come' to Kirkwall with me, nor did I see him that day. On New Year's Eve, bending to lift a heavy pile of papers out of the bottom drawer of a satinwood chest, I felt an intense spasm of pain in my back. After crawling upstairs on all fours, I spent the turn of the year in bed with a hot water bottle and a glass of Laphroaig: 'At midnight the Pole Star and other boats in the harbour sounded their fog horns and I drank whisky and did not mind being alone . . . it was better than the loneliness of being with people you don't really want to be with.'

3

AMONG THE SHADOWS

George is mentioned hardly at all in my diary during the first couple of weeks in January 1990, the absence of his name suggesting a coolness between us, although I rang him on New Year's Day to wish him well. Perhaps I hadn't succeeded in hiding from him the irritation I felt in December; perhaps I had hurt his feelings, being too self-absorbed to be sufficiently kind. I must still have been feeling under pressure, as I wrote 'JUST SAY NO' across the top of the pages for the first two weeks of 1990. On the evening of 2 January I was 'alone again. George not at home' – and yet these rather dispiriting words come at the end of a paragraph in which I described 'a lovely afternoon at the Gordons. Tea too. At Granny's before that.' Clearly my back injury from New Year's Eve had quickly mended. I also referred to 'John Broom & the terrible things that man has said & written', implying that his letter was still on my mind. On the 3rd I went for a long walk on the peat hill in Stenness and 'the view opened out in a way I would not have dreamed possible – both lochs; Skaill in the distance; all the shapes of the hills made clear'. Wanting to tell George about it, I rang him in the evening, but Renée was there and he did not suggest I went. I saw him the following day, however: 'at four I hurried home – took a piece of Catherine's birthday cake down to George[1] – ate soup and stroked the cat'. That meant that Nora was away again and George was minding Gypsy.

I was going out to dinner later that evening at Gloria and John Wallington's house ('the upstairs room so beautiful – light and warm and a roaring fire') and they also invited Keith Hobbs, known professionally as Keith Allardyce, a photographer and former lighthouse keeper who was based in Stromness for a while, living in a small house called Rockville that belonged to Bryce Wilson (who was then Orkney's Museums Officer). I'd met Keith a few times but we didn't know one another well. He was busy working on the book *Sea Haven*, a photographic archive of Stromness, created over a single year, for which Bryce was writing the text and for which George would later write the foreword, but he found time to invite me to Rockville for a meal on the following Sunday. I asked him to dinner at Faravel in return, and thereafter we began meeting more frequently. I wasn't sure what George would think about this. I was aware that he already knew Keith, who had lived in Stromness before, in a house called The Grieveship that Nora referred to only half-jokingly as 'the Hovel'. (By one of life's coincidences, the house was later sold to David Simpson, who had first brought me to Orkney, but by that stage it needed a complete renovation – apparently some of Keith's friends were shocked by the conditions in which he lived.) Keith still remembers a visit to Birsay with George and Nora during the 1970s, when they went to look at a cottage where George had once stayed, called Hell: 'The next house across the field is called Purgatory. The roof was still on the house then, and an American stove was intact in one room. There was silence as we (GMB, Nora and myself) went in to look, except for the clicking of a battery supplying volts to an electric fence.'

Keith's recollection was that George had stayed at Hell when convalescing from TB, perhaps in the 1940s, but in Maggie Fergusson's biography she refers to the Browns having a family holiday there and mentions George's terror of the bulls on nearby land.[2] Because of this shared history with George and Nora, and the fact that sometimes we all met socially, it was inevitable that Keith's name should come up in my conversations with George, but I was unsure just how much I should say about the fact that I was spending quite a lot of time with him. I would have liked to discuss this new and sometimes unsettling state of affairs, but there were still constraints to our confidences, as there had always been.

The first few months of that year were a lively time – it was clear that my plan to 'just say no' and have a quieter life had been abandoned. During one week in January I went to an Arts Society meeting, a talk by the artist Colin Johnstone, a concert, a dinner with Keith and a lunch with Beverley, and there was little time left to spend with George. But on the following Sunday I gave him a lift to evening Mass, and on Tuesday there was a poetry reading of a rather different kind, 'nonsense verse: limericks and clerihews' by Peter Driver, who lived on the outskirts of Stromness. That was an evening full of mirth and enjoyment, just what was needed to lift the spirits. On Thursday, George went into hospital in Aberdeen again, but he came home a few days later and I rang him on the 30th to find out how he had fared. John Broom was also in hospital, in the Balfour in Kirkwall, and I went to visit him several times, trying to mend the situation between us. Granny was admitted to the Balfour too, so there was lots of driving to and fro at visiting times, and then there was an early morning run to take Keith to the airport for a trip to Edinburgh. George came to tea at Faravel twice in February and we spent two evenings together at Mayburn Court.

George's friend Moira Burgess was in Orkney in March, to give a reading at the Pier Arts Centre, and I invited George to have supper and a dram with us at Faravel beforehand. After the meal, Moira said that she must go and change her clothes. 'Putting on your bardic robes, Moira?' joked George. The reading went well and George reviewed it for *The Orcadian*, mentioning his amusement when a member of the audience claimed to have detected Moira's debt to the writer Frank O'Connor – whose work she had never read.[3] George wrote to her shortly afterwards: 'Your reading was much enjoyed in Stromness. The wretched weather limited the audience a bit. I did enjoy our meal and drink at Jo's house.' He was looking forward to her return in July, when she would be visiting Orkney with her children, and praised a poem that her son had written ('wonderfully good'), referring to Peter's 'innocent eye'. He went on to say that he had seen John Broom the previous day, 'on the road, and thought him improved – not having seen him for 2 weeks or so' and added 'Had a visit from Jo last night. We watched the film of *Maurice*, the posthumous E. M. Forster novel. The film was interesting but so dull, lacking the good narrative prose, compared to the original. I think *Maurice*, though good enough, is the least successful of Forster's novels. The other 5 I never tire of.'[4]

Early in April, George asked me if I would take him in the car to visit some friends of his, the artist Julio Brajuha, his wife, Valerie, and their young daughter, Bianca; they were renting a cottage along the Redland Road in the parish of Firth. We went on a bright but chilly Saturday afternoon and were able to sit outside – making sure that George was well wrapped in his coat and scarf – to drink tea amongst the daffodils before going indoors to look at some of Julio's paintings. The following morning George came up to Faravel and we set out again, so that I could deliver him to Our Lady and St Joseph's in Kirkwall before I went to St Magnus Cathedral for the morning service. Writing to my parents a few days later, I mentioned these outings and George's apparent state of mind:

> The weather is back to indifference after our glorious week-end . . . I was at Firth with George . . . wonderful blues & greens . . . George really enjoyed the weekend, & on the way back from church on Sunday he was talking about things we might do in the summer – so at least he's thinking positively . . . Now I'm off to have a cup of tea with George & Nora.

Despite his positive thinking, George was about to be sent back to hospital in Aberdeen. Perhaps he revealed his fears to other friends but with me he was stoical, seeming quietly resigned to this disruption and discomfort. He went away on 11 April, the day on which the Canadian poet Robert Bringhurst arrived to give a reading. I met Robert at the airport and took him out to dinner at the Scorrabrae Inn in Orphir, which was a place that George and I both liked, and I wished that George could have been with us.

George wrote to me from Ward 33, generous with his praise of a home-made card I'd sent him and referring in a characteristically low-key way to the blow he'd just received:

The photo of Stromness with the first lights coming on is very beautiful. Now you'll have to consider an exhibition and/or a book of your pictures . . .

A lovely morning in Aberdeen, sun coming through the sea-haar, and I must languish in this sanitised tower a bit longer it seems.

I got slightly disturbing news yesterday: that I'll have to undergo 2 operations, both fairly major, sometime soon.

Orkney at this time of year is all I desire – and my work – but those 2 bridges will have to be crossed, if I amn't [sic] to be lost in the marsh . . . I keep quite cheerful, outwardly . . .

Now I have a quiet ward without TV – not even radio. I have sketched out a few poems over the past ten days.

I'll phone later, Jo. Best regards to all our friends.

Looking forward to have lunch with you in the Scorrabrae before midsummer. I hope Billie isn't getting into any fights, but acting ladylike.[5]

A second letter acknowledged the horrible time he had been having:

I suppose I have been 'through the mill' as they say: anyway, taken a little bruising from the millstones. From now on things should improve. I have to have, still, a third smaller operation, maybe in 2 weeks' time.

How very much I miss Orkney in May! I always loved the

springing light, rising higher and higher towards the solstice. I do hope to be home for June. I do hope to share a meal with you, Jo.

But now I know you're to be in Aberdeen next weekend. Peter and Betty will be glad to see you, and of course I will too.

Remember me to all our Orkney friends. Have you heard from Keith? My best regards to him.

To estimate my condition these 2½ weeks: I haven't wanted to read or listen to music or watch TV, and have eaten little and listlessly, and had trouble sleeping. Now all these things are beginning to come right.

Enjoy the beginning of summer, Jo. Is Billie being good? God bless.[6]

As he anticipated, I was able to visit him because I was in Aberdeen for a one-day library conference on Saturday 19 May, and I saw him on Sunday afternoon, finding my way through the maze of corridors to a small, white room (so different from the cosy clutter of Mayburn Court) where George lay smiling up at me. Peter and Betty Grant invited me for a meal at their house in Broomhill Road in the evening and were as kind and hospitable as always. George wrote again on the 24th:

It was lovely, your visit last Sunday; it brought Orkney and all its springtime airs into this little ward.

How I long to be in Stromness just now, with the light growing and the wild flowers coming in profusion.

May your car soon be healed, Jo, so we can have that supper at Scorrabrae: if we can get inside for tourists, for the season will soon be upon us.

9.30 this morning I had to go for another skin graft, skilfully & quickly & almost painlessly done . . . I've just had
communion from a nun, sister Jean, this being Ascension day.

Any moment I expect to hear Peter Grant's footsteps
coming Betty will come in the evening. They enjoyed your
visit last Sunday very much.

Very light reading these days: John Mortimer's *Rumpole
of the Old Bailey* . . .

A patient next door puts the TV on too loud – I've
protested once today. It's such a strange life here, compared
to Stromness: one droops sometimes, though surrounded by
healing and kindness.

My kind regards to all our friends. Give Billie a stroke for
me, and a pat and a scratch under the chin . . .

Be well and happy, Jo.

The most dreaded times here are the twice-a-day dressings.
But once they're over, we all feel a small victory has been won.

Much love, George XX.[7]

My car was having hefty repairs that week, and when I received
a very surprising telephone call from my bank to tell me that an
anonymous well-wisher had deposited £200 in my account to
pay the garage bill, I suspected that George was my benefactor.
I knew he sometimes helped Nora when she was in financial
difficulty and this gesture seemed in keeping with his generous
nature. I wrote to him in some embarrassment to ask if he was
the mysterious donor, and to thank him – but no. 'Thank you
for 2 lovely letters', he wrote. 'I'm very pleased your car is on
the road again. That anonymous gift is wonderful. It wasn't
me, Jo (I wish I'd thought of it). You have many dear friends. A

lovely early morning through the ward window. I'm beginning to repine in here. The day of release is uncertain yet.'[8]

He was still having a grim time. Not only had he undergone an operation the previous Tuesday, but he was to have his remaining teeth extracted the following week. 'Not much left of me to come home!' he joked. 'I wrote some verse but that has dried up temporarily. I think I'll pass the time this weekend writing a story for young folk, but I don't yet know the theme.' These last words were somehow immensely reassuring. There he was, having surgery and teeth extractions, far from home, yet he could still write creatively. He was also still taking an interest in other people's problems. He knew that I had been struggling at the Academy recently, finding myself increasingly unable to deal single-handedly with the large numbers of lively teenagers who surged in before school and during lunchtimes to use the library for recreation rather than study. 'May things have settled down in your library, Jo', he wrote solicitously. 'The library is your sovereign territory: exert all your rights and privileges.' He went on:

Quiet in hospital now at 6.30. In ¾ hour it will suddenly rouse like a beehive, and so continue until lights out.

The Grants continue to be wonderful in every way.

I hope the weather is saving up its sunshine for your parents' visit. I do hope to see them . . . Nora was here last weekend. She came from visiting Simon Fraser the artist and publisher. I hope Billie is well. The Bevans have a new kitten.

Surely I'll see you before the end of June. Much love.

Then there was a later postscript: 'It seems now I'll be going to Orkney on Monday or Tuesday but to Balfour to begin with.

The arduous business of dressing wounds will go on for a little while. Glad, though, to be in Orkney.'

These letters were comforting, but I found that it was disconcerting to be in Stromness without George in residence at Mayburn Court. I wrote to my parents on 19 June, saying that 'things are busy in one sense with school and lots of meetings, but socially it's a bit odd, with George not having been at home for so long, and Beverley away until September, and Keith not back until October . . . I hope George will be home by the time you come, but Dr Rae [Colin Rae, at the Stromness surgery] wants to keep him in hospital until after the Festival because he's afraid George will go out and tire himself.' Now that the *Sea Haven* project had been completed, Keith was away on the mainland, working on a new commission, although he did return to Orkney from time to time.

The St Magnus Festival would certainly have meant an increase in the number of visitors climbing the Mayburn Court steps to call on George, and the Stromness street would have been bustling with tourists. Liz Lochhead, the festival poet, came to give a reading at the Pier Arts Centre on 23 June, and my parents arrived in Orkney a few days later, by which time George was safely back, and we spent the afternoon with him on the 30th. The following month was almost as busy: 'Monday 9 July: Phone calls: Allison Dixon re. drinks Thurs – GMB, Murrays, Jim.' Moira Burgess was in Orkney again and came for coffee one morning, before I set off at 4 o'clock (in a gale, with some trepidation) to Papa Westray for an overnight stay, as the soprano Emma Kirkby and the lutenist Anthony Rooley (who founded and directs the Consort of Musicke) were giving a concert at Holland Farm. I sailed back to Kirkwall on the

MV *Orcadia* to find that Keith had arrived at Faravel, and we were going that evening for drinks with George and the Dixons at Langskaill. I had never been to the house before, and it was good to see the place where George spent so many happy times. Keith left Orkney again the following night, on the MV *St Sunniva*.

When Keith was away, George often asked if I'd heard from him and was always affectionately sympathetic when I replied (as I frequently did) that I hadn't received so much as a postcard. Yet if ever I ventured to speak more candidly about my emotions, a different expression would cross George's face – an expression that suggested he was not interested in hearing about this and regarded it as a private matter – and eventually I learned to keep quiet. Certainly I never felt able to ask George about his own intimate relationships; I was afraid of that reproving look, the one that said I had trespassed. I knew very little then about the women he had loved, although when he first spoke to me about Nora it was with a warmth that left me in no doubt of his lasting affection for her. At that stage I had never even heard of his great love, Stella Cartwright (George didn't mention her to me, nor did his friends – I knew nothing about her until I read his autobiography, after his death), and although he occasionally talked admiringly and enthusiastically about Kenna Crawford, he didn't make it clear that he had felt much more for her than friendship. It was a revelation to read fragments of the loving, longing letters he wrote to her, quoted in Maggie Fergusson's biography of George.[9] His reserve, in speaking of matters of the heart, meant that I never knew what he felt about my relationship with Keith. During the summer, however, Keith seemed to be moving on, in every sense, and it is evident from passages in my notebook that as matters drew to a rather painful conclusion, George and I found ourselves more comfortable with one another again. 'Alison, Beverley, Chris [Meek] . . . all away', I wrote on 22 July. 'But the evening was blessed with GMB's company & golden light over Skaill.'

That was one bright evening in a season of shadows. Apart from the fact that the black dog was on my shoulder again, we were all worrying about John Broom. He had been admitted to the Balfour Hospital in Kirkwall after suffering a severe stroke that had robbed him of his inhibitions, and during my visits to him I found his conversation very coarse; I noted in my diary that Betty Grant had also been taken aback by John's language when she saw him. I felt desperately sorry for him, aware that he couldn't help himself, but it was not easy to be in his company. I talked to George about this, mentioning a small and rather distressing incident that had happened on my second visit to John and wondering aloud whether I would be able to face visiting him again. George was perturbed and sympathetic, but although it has been claimed that he 'disowned' John after his stroke,[10] that isn't quite how I remember it. George's poem 'In Memoriam John L. Broom' is not especially affectionate, but it is respectful, and does not suggest to me that the friendship had been broken; there is also an acknowledgement that John's life had not been easy:

> In sorrow the bread and salt are eaten.
> [. . .]
> The feast and the dance
> Are more beautiful
> For that road of thorns and stones.[11]

Someone – it might have been George – lent me a book that John had written, under the pseudonym Abraham Adams, titled *Another Little Drink: The Story of an Alcoholic's Decline, Fall and Return to Life*,[12] and I hoped that reading it might enable me to understand him a little better, but I'm not sure that it helped very much, other than to confirm that John was a complicated man.

I decided that it would be good to go away for a while, and booked a trip to Shetland for August, arranging to stay for a week on the island of Foula and a few days in Lerwick. In the meantime I tried to keep myself occupied, with an outing to the uninhabited island of Eynhallow, and a trip to Graemsay on a glorious day with a sky of Mediterranean blue. Aileen Paterson, the author of the 'Maisie' books for children, came to Orkney in July, and after meeting her at the airport I took her to Radio Orkney's offices to be interviewed before a storytelling session in Stromness. 'She was wonderful with the children', I noted, and she captivated the adults too when she gave a talk about her writing on the following evening.

I saw little of George for the next few weeks because he was busy with visitors from the mainland. Paddy Hughes was in Orkney and so were Peter and Betty Grant. I visited Mayburn Court one evening when the Grants were staying there, but found it 'curiously depressing ... We sat in the dark (it was raining again) and drank gin and tonic, and George scarcely spoke.' On 31 July I woke up 'to a feeling of terror' and next day I wrote about a sense of desperation and failure. I copied out a passage from Rosamond Lehmann's novel *Dusty Answer* (1927) which sheds light on my state of mind at that time: 'She was rid at last of the weakness, the futile obsession of dependence on other people. She had nobody now except herself, and that was best . . . This was to be happy – this emptiness, this light coloured state, this no-thought and no-feeling.' I couldn't have been an easy companion at that time, and if George was struggling with depression as well as with serious physical illness then it is not surprising that communication between us sometimes faltered, although I had no idea then of the extent of his suffering.

From time to time I asked myself whether I had misunderstood the nature of George's feelings towards me. From our second meeting onwards he had always greeted me and parted from me with a kiss, but these kisses seemed to be tokens of affectionate friendship and nothing more than that. A young pupil at the Academy – a relation of George's – came into the library one day and rather shocked me by asking, without much preamble, 'When are you going to marry George?' I couldn't help wondering whether the child had heard the subject discussed at home. But marriage would surely have been unthinkable for George, even if his affection for me amounted to more than I realised, because he was a devout Catholic and I had been divorced some years before coming to Orkney. It was unthinkable for me too, because my affection for George did not tend that way. Apart from returning his kisses, and holding his hand in a taxi after we had both had a dram or two at the Braes Hotel, the most physically intimate thing I had ever done for him was to cut his fingernails, after he admitted one day that he found it difficult and would like some help. I found such supposition – about the possibility of our marriage – distressing, just as I was upset by the grumblings of John Broom, who liked to imply that my relationship with George was a romantic one.

George's apparent enjoyment of my company was flattering, but although the great gap between our ages would not necessarily have been an impediment to a different kind of closeness, he understood (because I had never made a secret of it) that I longed to marry again and to have a child.

George had a wonderful rapport with his young great-nephews and great-nieces, as Ron Ferguson's interview with Allison Dixon makes clear,[13] and he took a tremendous interest in his friends' children – this is evident from his letters to Moira Burgess, for example, in which he often writes about her children, Kirsten and Peter Stirling, and in our conversations he often mentioned Peter and Betty Grant's son, Alan. But in view of George's need for the kind of solitude and silence in which he could write for at least three hours each day, and his settled habits, it is hard to imagine that he would seriously have contemplated marriage and domesticity at that point in his life.

To this day, I have no clear idea how much speculation there was about what George and I felt for one another, although someone claimed quite recently that it was a common perception that we were lovers. This is a small town, and we were often seen together; it would have been known that I spent many evenings at Mayburn Court. But most of the people who loved him best seemed to understand matters perfectly – or at least as well as I understood them myself.

I was touched when George rang early on the morning of my departure for Shetland at the beginning of August, to wish me well for my journey – and what a journey it was, with Fair Isle seen on the horizon from the deck of the MV *St Sunniva*, and a first glimpse of Foula's hills from the window of an eight-seater plane. I spent hours on Foula walking and thinking, having vivid dreams at night, and writing compulsively, scribbling notes about place names and birds and wild flowers, and making drafts of poems. The Kame is one of the highest cliffs in Europe, and the drama of the landscape helped to put things into perspective; the peace and austere beauty of the island worked their healing power. I put the time to some practical use, too: my kind hosts at Leraback, Marian and Brian, encouraged me to visit their friend Penny Millsopp, who gave tuition in spinning at the croft where she lived with her family. Thus, one morning, I went to sit in her workshop at Broadfoot, 'lit with the sun & the warm golden colour of wood & the rich hues of mounds of dyed fleece' heaped up beside a loom, and I learned the rudiments of teasing out, carding and spinning a fleece.

Penny was skilled and patient, and even in a single day I made some progress. At lunchtime she gave me home-made soup and bread and told me some of her life story, and at the end of the school day I saw her daughters playing outside and heard them calling to one another on the hill. Those memories stayed with me – 'by meeting one person, horizons broaden & something disproportionately important is learned, gained', I wrote – and I shared them later with George. I told him, too, about the fierce Bonxies, the great skuas, which gathered menacingly and then attacked if they felt their chicks were in danger, swooping down suddenly: 'one Bonxie swooped madly, shrieking wildly, over & over – suddenly I saw the female, running to the left of me, trailing her wing, & sure enough, a few yards ahead there was a large, soft, indignant chick in its nest.' Brian lent me a stick to wave above my head – a shepherd's crook, I think – to protect myself, and I was glad of it as I heard the whoosh of wings pass close above me. George listened to my stories and wove some of them into my next birthday acrostic.

I left Foula on 14 August and spent a few days in Lerwick, in a small and not very nice guest house which smelt of burnt toast. 'It's raining, dismal, & I'm cross', I complained in my notebook – though not to my landlady. She seemed a rather dependent person, and having discovered that I had hired a car she soon got me running errands, collecting her prescriptions and taking her to the shops. 'The closing in of other people's needs', I wrote despairingly, thinking of some of the commitments I faced when I returned home, although it was clear that I didn't regard seeing George as in any way a duty – I mentioned my 'real pleasure' in being with him, adding 'but not even to have two weeks without demands!'

Earlier that day I had driven to St Ninian's Isle, from where I saw the jagged blue outline of Foula in the distance: 'I realised that I'd been thinking of a place in the past, or in dreams, lost forever . . . After St Ninian's, I went to Hamnavoe, partly to tell George I'd been.' On the way back to Lerwick I took a detour and stopped beside Tingwall Loch, where I listened to a sung Mass on the car radio, again thinking of George – a 'great purity of sound'. Keith rang me at the guest house but he sounded very far away. I woke early next morning with 'the stomach-turning dread that I associate with London & cold bedsits . . . I want to be safely back on my island.' Nevertheless, I had one very happy evening in Lerwick when I was invited to the home of the author Rhoda Bulter and her husband. They were marvellous hosts and I stayed for several hours; George's name inevitably came into our conversation about writers and writing. We hoped that Rhoda might one day come to

Stromness to give a reading, but sadly this was never possible (she died in 1994).

Donald and Dorrie came to meet me off the boat in Stromness and I went to their house for 'tea and whisky and the News' – a great deal seemed to have happened in Stromness in my absence. 'Donald took me home, & there was my lovely house again', I wrote. 'But after a moment the telephone rang.' My friend and colleague Jim Lawson was calling to say that he was on his way up to the Braes Hotel and wondered if I needed bread and milk, but instead of going to the pub he came in for a dram and we talked until the early hours.

I found myself quickly reabsorbed into Stromness life. I often walked round the West Shore in the evening, for we had a spell of good weather: 'Stenness peat hill is purple, gold & green', I wrote on 25 August, 'handfuls of light thrown down.' I went up to the Braes Hotel with Jim once or twice, and Elizabeth and Grenville Gore-Langton invited me to go with George to lunch at Garth. I had been there once before, for cocktails (as George's chauffeur on that occasion, because he needed someone to drive him), and Tam and Gunnie had been amongst the guests – I remember Gunnie looking stunning in a silky green kaftan. At this lunch there were five of us: Elizabeth, Grenville, Theresia (a friend who was staying at Garth), George and I:

Saturday . . . home to change for lunch with the Countess; Garth – the furniture & lamps & mirrors – Limoges china (white, with a pattern of green leaves) – their German visitor, Theresia . . . E. G.-L. talking about her hairdo for the Queen Mother's party . . . an enormous fresh salmon, baked in buttered paper – potatoes taken from the ground

two hours ago – peas – meringues, raspberries, cream . . .
The sun was bright through their huge window – patches of
silvery light on a very calm sea below the Kame of Hoy – hills
of Sutherland partly visible. At 5 we left . . . & I took George
to Warebeth for a walk (Gunnie swimming).

Meals seemed to feature quite a lot in my diary at this time:
'Monday [27 August] – Dad's birthday . . . An early tea with
GMB – Susie Johnstone's meat pie. Renée came so I left early
(but felt kindly towards her . . .).' I also mentioned a Sunday
lunch with Irene Traill Thomson, who had introduced herself
to me at the Episcopal church in Stromness and often invited
me to her house on one of the piers for a glass of sherry or a
meal 'at her table which seems practically on the water'.

I saw George again on 1 September: 'At seven – blasts of
golden light, too bright to bear, & purple clouds over Scapa
Flow . . . And GMB rang at this point, asking if he could come
to Kirkwall with me – slight rearrangement of plans but it will
be fine – I'm glad of it.' Later I added that it had been 'an
odd, panic-stricken sort of day, when I felt out of kilter with all
the world. But George did come & we got safely to Kirkwall.'
We did some shopping and took his watch to Hourston's the
jeweller's to be repaired, meeting Marjorie Linklater on the
way. I also described how I had felt 'last night, beside his fire,
drinking tea and talking nineteen to the dozen about Foula, &
the permissive society, it was just like old times – he hugged
me closely when I arrived and when I left – talked to me about
his will – I hope I conveyed to him that I want nothing, expect
nothing from him.'

This slightly evasive mention of George's will referred to the fact that he had confided his idea of leaving his house to me. He brought up the subject quite casually over a cup of tea, much as if he were speaking of leaving me a collection of books or a painting, saying that his relations had homes of their own and would perhaps not want to be bothered with Mayburn Court, which suggested an astonishing naivety on his part. His home had been built as a council house but he was in the process of buying it, and the purchase was finalised in November that year.[14] He referred to it once as 'a kind of watchtower house';[15] it was actually a two-bedroom maisonette on two floors but there was another single-storey flat below, so it was quite high up, and sometimes the occupant of the lower flat would thump on her ceiling with a broom if George and his visitors were making too much noise or his television was too loud. A steep flight of steps outside led up to the balcony that George describes briefly in the poem 'An Old Man in July':

> Lucent rain-bubbles
> Burst on the pools of his balcony
> And a sparrow
> Eyes from the rusted railing
> Bits of bread an old man scatters.[16]

When George raised this question of whether I would like Mayburn Court to pass to me when he died, I was shocked, and all kinds of thoughts went buzzing around inside my head. For one thing, it was hard to confront the possibility of George's death in the foreseeable future; for another, there were practical considerations. George was closer to some members of his family than to others, and therefore to leave the house to an outsider would have avoided a possible dilemma, although of course it could simply have been sold and the proceeds shared out. I imagined that if his relations – not to mention his close friends – discovered his plan to bequeath his house to me they would be appalled, justifiably misconstruing the nature of our friendship, or suspecting that I had persuaded George to this course of action, although that could not have been further from the truth. I could easily picture the furore in my own family if one of my uncles were to leave his house to a woman whom he had known for only two years.

In one sense it was wonderful to know that George wanted to do this for me; it suggested a truly solicitous affection. But even if there had been no other reasons for demurring, I loved my rented house at Faravel, for its lightness and its view of the Orphir hills. My tenancy was secure for as long as I stayed in post as school librarian, and although I sometimes found my job surprisingly difficult I had no plans to move on. I still owned my two-roomed flat in east London, which I rented out when I moved to Orkney and which had become an endless source of worry, so another flat or house seemed to be the last thing I needed just then. I tried to explain all this to George and we talked about it for the rest of the evening, including the possibility that Nora might inherit 3 Mayburn Court, as he worried so much about her precarious financial situation.

I never saw George's will, but Geoffrey Elborn explained in Nora's obituary that her importance in George's life was publicly obvious because he left her a life interest in his house (which would then pass to a relative after her death). Elborn also suggested – and with reason – that this had 'caused local controversy', although it could be argued that it was a good compromise on George's part: he was doing something for Nora and yet also acknowledging his family's claims. But 3 Mayburn Court stood empty for many months after George's death, and its unlit windows were a source of sadness to me as I walked past. I began to think that the house had become a worry for Nora, rather than a blessing, and it might also have seemed a forlorn place, once emptied of George's possessions, which passed to his family. It was eventually sold and now, more than twenty years later, still stands unlit and apparently empty for most of the year, though a blue plaque marks the fact that George once lived there.

As the summer visitors went away, fragments from my account of September show that George and I soon slipped back into our old habits of meetings and outings. I called on an elderly friend, Jessie Mowat, and then went on to George's for a dram one evening; I made date shortbread for him; I wondered how I would celebrate my birthday: 'If at all – presumably not with Alison, who will probably have a rehearsal for the community play. With George, perhaps.' I noted with pleasure that he was 'his old self'.

These were mostly calm and happy times, although another shadow was cast by the indomitable Renée. George telephoned me on 12 September with the usual warm invitation for tea and cake, but when I arrived I could tell that there was something he wanted to tell me, and after a while he hesitantly confided that he had been upset by something that she had said. 'Renée unpleasant about *me*?' I noted later. 'Or so it seemed.' George was reluctant to repeat her words but he gave me the gist of them. Both Nora and I were divorcees, and I had always understood from George's hints that Renée considered us to be unworthy of his regard, perhaps little better than ladies of the night – Ron Ferguson's tactful way of putting it was that Renée thought Nora was 'up to no good'.[17] It therefore came as no great surprise to hear that she had openly expressed her disapproval – it is possible, I suppose, that she subscribed to the view that George and I were lovers. But George was at pains to show me how much he minded whatever it was that she had said. The next day, I wrote: 'Small details – George's affection on the telephone, defying Renée. A wild wind tonight – winter stars – fierce glow over Flotta.' I was never quite able to reconcile Renée's attitude towards me with the fact that she – an unmarried woman as far as I knew – had a child of her own, and grandchildren.

I wondered sometimes whether it was difficult for George to keep the peace between his friends and relations, and Brian Murray recently mentioned an occasion when George had walked out of Renée's house, taking Surinder with him, because of something offensive she said about a member of George's family. There was certainly little love lost between Renée and myself, and between Renée and Nora. Allison Dixon hinted that she and Fraser found themselves in need of some diplomacy each year when they invited both Renée and Nora to accompany George to Christmas lunch at Langskaill (Allison confirmed this in her conversation with Ron Ferguson when he interviewed her for his book).[18] Later on, after I remarried, Renée's attitude towards me changed, although I rarely found her an easy companion: she was forthright in her opinions and seemed unafraid to offend. As Maggie Fergusson puts it in Renée's obituary, 'Simm did not mince her words.'[19] She also had a maddening habit of pretending she hadn't heard, when she didn't like something I had said, although she seemed perfectly able to grasp the rest of the conversation. There were a few occasions when I set out for Mayburn Court and then turned back when I saw Renée's distinctive blue car parked nearby – she drove a Citroën 2CV and tended to drive in the middle of the road, to the alarm of other motorists, and there was a certain amount of schadenfreude when a story went round that she had reversed into a police car.

On other evenings, if I was in a more feisty mood, I would go and knock on George's door in spite of having seen her car, realising that he sometimes mischievously invited me when he knew perfectly well that she would be there. Whatever my view of her, however, there is no doubt that she completely adored George and that their visits to one another were important to both of them. Fergusson suggests in the obituary that George found Renee's company 'invigorating'. I was interested, however, to learn from George that he was not the first of her heroes. He told me that she had been a great admirer of the potter Bernard Leach (she owned many pieces of his work), and the obituary makes reference to the high regard she had for the artist William Lamb, whom she regarded as 'a model of what a true artist should be: unconcerned with worldly success, utterly dedicated to his craft', which could also have been said of George.[20]

George certainly had the gift of making people feel that he was indispensable to their happiness. London seemed as distant as another planet now; I was deeply immersed in Orkney life, and George was such an intrinsic part of my new world that I dreaded anything happening to him:

15 September. 8 a.m. Wonderful blue & gold sunrise at seven. Last night, after tea, I fell into a state of half sleep, half despair . . . terrified of a future in which anything changes.

16 September, 8 a.m. And again, beautiful early light . . . Billie is sitting on the warm sill, washing & pulling out her fur . . . And I must write about yesterday, because in small ways it was a very wonderful day, to be remembered always, distilling all the things I love most about living here, & in spite of the passing anxieties . . . I was happy & serene. A quality of light & warmth & feeling that I can't set down.

I went on to describe a visit to Ottersgill, the Kirklands' house in Stenness. I was continuing my attempts at spinning, teaching myself from a manual, and George often inquired about my progress. I had bought my own wheel and someone had given me a beautiful Jacob's fleece, which Donella offered to help me prepare for carding and spinning:

We sat outside, & she gave me spinning books to read, & made tea . . . & we laid my fleece out on the flagstones & looked at the diagram, & pondered, & eventually took it apart & put it into bags, variously labelled 'Legs', 'Sides – good', 'Neck – best', etc., & then – all the while there was this marvellous golden light, & warmth – I was in a cotton shirt with the sleeves rolled up – we went inside & drank sherry. And I kept thinking . . . how lucky I am to be here . . . to be living in this beautiful place.

In the early evening, Donella and I walked on the beach below the house, and there were seals in the water. It was a life I could never have anticipated – a rather extraordinary life for someone who had grown up in the suburbs of London – but I loved it, and I drove home:

> Feeling ecstatic about Orkney & my life in it . . . at 9, George rang, slightly plaintive, asking me down – so I went & it was lovely, the room cosy with a fire, & he was lively & we spoke of books, & all that he had been doing. If life could always be like this! But even as I talked to him & looked around that so-familiar room in the firelight, I knew that it could all end at any moment . . . & these evenings would never happen any more . . . Beverley's marriage and departure have made me see how ephemeral it all is.

On 18 August, the day after I returned from Shetland, Beverley had married Torben, a Danish archaeologist, and she moved to Denmark. I was truly happy for Beverley but I missed her very much. Alison Blacklock was busy with her job and two growing sons; Keith was more or less out of my life; and after all George's time in hospital I was only too well aware of how tenuous his hold on life was. Sometimes I felt that things might fall apart. In the meantime, George and I went on as we always had, and even when he was away there was no need to be lonely. Irene Traill Thomson invited me to her house on the day before my birthday and had prepared 'a wonderful tea for me . . . & there were two rainbows, high & graceful, as we sat by the sea windows'.

Peter Grant and Paddy Hughes were in Orkney that week, and I wrote about meeting them in the street after the opening of an exhibition of work by John Cumming, but George

nevertheless found time to come up to Faravel to celebrate
my birthday with me, as I had hoped: 'a fine day . . . I do not
mean the weather, which was dark & unremittingly wet . . .
in the evening George came to tea & brought me an acrostic
. . . a rush to get tea ready (tho' I'd spent the previous evening
cooking) – & what should I wear? And because of the wild rain
I went to fetch George in the car. Keith rang during tea.' After I
had taken George home – he didn't like late nights – I went to
the Braes Hotel with Alison, and Jim came up to join us. People
kept buying me whisky because it was my birthday so I had to
leave the car there, '& in a powerful cold wonderful wind we
walked down the hill. Next morning, after the worst night of
gale, perhaps, since I came here, the garden was blackened as
if by a prairie fire, the leaves twisted & dead, shrubs almost
uprooted.' George's acrostic was the one that alluded to my
Shetland journey:

Jo, you've gone to
Other islands northwards this summer
And Foula especially, and
Now you know all about the fierce Samurai, the bonxies,
Now you know how to draw
A fine thread of wool from a Shetland fleece.

Returning home is always good, although
Academy walls loom,
Morning to evening the light lessens, but still
September, stook-crowned, is the year's sovereign.
Enter, soon, the equinox,
Year's perfect equilibrium; but before that, this special day.

I found it difficult to stop blethering about Foula, but fortunately George seemed happy to listen. He hadn't been to the island himself but had seen other parts of Shetland on his holiday in 1988 with Gunnie, Kulgin and Colin, and he easily understood my delight. I was still spinning the Jacob's fleece and knitting it into a warm jacket, and I made a poem ('For Penny, on Foula'[21]) out of some of my Shetland notes. I was beginning to write more poetry and to send a few things off; I knew that some of George's earliest poems had appeared in *The New Shetlander* so I tried my luck there, and one day towards the end of September I came home to find a large envelope containing a copy of the magazine with two of my poems in it, together with a letter from the editors saying that they had used the pieces I sent and would be pleased to receive more. I was absurdly emotional: 'I burst into tears, because there was no one to share this with.' Wanting to tell someone who would understand, 'I rushed along the street (it was 9.30) to have a cup of tea with George, as promised . . . Who has a cold . . . (And confessed to him about the poems).' And of course he asked to see them; I felt shy about showing them to him but he was kind and encouraging. Over the next few years he often asked about what I was writing, but I was hesitant about letting him see my work because I was always afraid that he would feel he had to find something nice to say.

George's own latest publication was *Letters to Gypsy* and he had previously asked if it was all right to mention me in it – he was always meticulous about making sure I had no objection to appearing in anything he wrote, even if it was a brief mention in 'Under Brinkie's Brae'. I saw the new book when I went down to watch television with him: 'Tuesday – to GMB – *Barchester*

Chronicles[22] & a gift of cakes . . . dear George. He showed me a copy of Gypsy's book – Billie & I are in it.' Later he gave me a copy, signing it 'To Jo and Billie with love from George and Gypsy, Christmas 1990'. *Letters to Gypsy* comprises a selection of the letters that George had been writing for many years to Nora's cat, and it reveals that wonderfully playful aspect of George's nature that I found so endearing. He loved cats, but not dogs: 'I take care to avoid mentioning dogs whenever possible in my writing', he declared once in 'Under Brinkie's Brae'. 'If they *have* to appear, a sinister aura clings about them. I would never think of joining a Dog Lovers' Society. With cats, it's quite another matter.'[23] He was rather shocked when he received a request from the Scottish writer Maurice Lindsay, asking him to contribute to an anthology of poems about dogs, and declined the invitation, saying that his muse 'had a marked aversion to writing about dogs', which he attributed to having been attacked by a dog when he was a small child. Lindsay, however, pointed out that the poem didn't actually have to be in praise of dogs, and so 'now something will happen that I'd have thought impossible a month ago – I'm to be in a collection of dog poems'.[24]

George had been 'enchanted by cats since infancy' and he always liked to have Billie on his lap when he came to Faravel. She had appeared outside my London flat one day and refused to go away, and when I eventually traced her owner, the woman told me that she was moving house and asked if I could give the cat a permanent home. Thus, when I moved to Orkney, Billie had to come too. She settled quite happily into her new life, although she was alarmed when she first saw cows in a field close to Faravel, and I soon discovered that she couldn't bear to be

left, even for a few days. No matter what careful arrangements
I made for her – either at the cattery, or with kind neighbours
coming in to feed her – she developed a habit of pulling out
her fur if I was away, and all the vet's attempts to remedy this
problem had been in vain. George mentioned it in two of his
letters to Gypsy. One was 'Billie Ramsey's Behaviour':

> You must have heard about Billie Ramsey the Faravel cat. Well,
> Billie was lonely when Joanna her mother was in Aberdeen last
> weekend . . . I saw Billie at her front door, hoping (like me)
> that the sun would come out warm and bright. "Hello Billie",
> I called from the steps. Billie looked through me as though I
> was made of glass . . . By the way, Billie had left little tufts of
> her fur all over the carpet. *"Look how clever I am, decorating the
> living-room for you while you've been away."*

The other letter was 'Consolation in Loneliness': 'Another
lonely cat today, until next Monday, is Billie Ramsey, because
her mother is flying to London. When Joanna comes back, what
will she find? Tufts and puff-balls and rags of fur everywhere.'[25]

At the end of September I went across to Hoy on a
Friday evening, to a concert described in my diary as 'Max's
composers', referring to an event which was the culmination of
one of the Hoy Summer Schools at which Max taught young
composers.[26] A group of us (but not George, who stayed at
home that evening) sat together on the MV *Jessie Ellen*:

> Dorrie & Donald; Brian T . . . in a very daring mood – Dick
> H . . . smoking a cigar – Jane G., to whom I was cold &
> not friendly. At some point – during the concert's interval, I

think – I saw her looking a little lost, & felt a small pang of guilt. But after her manipulation & exploitation of George this week – [her friend] filming him or getting [him] to read onto a tape or suchlike – the whole story too tedious – I owe her no kindness . . . Coming back the air wasn't cold & I sat outside & watched the lights of Flotta like a visionary city floating on the water . . . We went round the far side of Graemsay, by Hoy High, because of rough seas.

Reading this rather evasive entry again after many years, I realise how protective I sometimes felt of George. The incident in question involved a request from an acquaintance that I should try to persuade George to be interviewed by a friend of hers. When I mentioned it to him – reluctantly, for I was fairly sure I could guess the outcome – he was unhappy about it and eventually said he would rather not do it. But the friend had disregarded his refusal and turned up at his house, apparently insistent, and I was furious.

For most of September, however, I seem to have felt calm and more settled: 'How I love these relaxed Saturdays', I wrote at the end of the month. 'I think of the dreary trek up Leytonstone High Road . . . Stromness is so beautiful (as I went down the path it had just stopped raining but the sky was a deep grey & there was a wonderful smell of peat smoke & seaweed & crabs) . . . tea with Mrs TT [Traill Thomson] . . . her room washed in sun & sealight.'

October began with a reading by the novelist Alanna Knight at the Pier Arts Centre, which was a delightful evening, and the following night I went to the Stromness community play. George's name recurs through my account of that month: 'And

Sunday . . . coming back past Skaill and walking the beach as
the sun set in splendour at the headland . . . And in the evening
. . . I went, rather late, to have a cup of tea with dear George,
who is always the same, & never changes in his affection.' There
are small prosaic details – 'Yesterday: Kirkwall . . . back by one
& down to George's with his frozen mince' – as well as brief
mentions of more special times: 'A strange, full, chaotic week
. . . the party at Gunnie's for Gypsy . . . St Magnus – a bright
sunny drive with George & Brian Murray & coming back past
Orphir' (the party was the launch of *Letters to Gypsy*). On Sunday
the 14th I went to 'St Magnus – with George and Murrays' and
on Tuesday, the day before George's birthday, I saw him in the
evening for a dram. There was another launch, for *Sea Haven*,
at the Pier Arts Centre on the following Saturday, which meant
that Keith was back in Orkney for a few days, and there was a
buzz of excitement in Stromness because this beautiful book
was all about our town, its features and its leading characters
skilfully photographed and eloquently described.

   During the following week I drove up to Birsay one evening
to collect George from a family celebration at the Barony Hotel.
The party should have been a pleasant prospect for him, but when
he mentioned it to me it was clear that something was troubling
him. His nephew Erlend had offered to drive him there and
home again, but by that stage in George's life he liked to be back
beside his own fire at a reasonable hour. He fretted that Erlend's
evening would be spoilt if he had to leave early, and although
Erlend said he would happily take George home and then return
to the party, making no difficulty at all about it, George hated
to feel he was being a bother. I said I could easily collect him
whenever he wanted, and was rewarded by seeing his face light

up with relief. We agreed on the time that I should arrive, and he was able to look forward to the party without misgivings.

I refrained from telling George that I was slightly unsure if I would be able to find the Barony in the dark, not knowing the Birsay roads very well, but I arrived without mishap. The barman directed me up to the room where the party was being held and I peered in at the door: there, amidst a convivial group, sat George, engrossed and happy, obviously enjoying himself. Someone noticed me and invited me to join the throng but, apart from being rather too casually dressed for a party, I felt I would be out of place at this family occasion and went down to the bar, where I spent a peaceful hour reading a book and drinking orange juice and eavesdropping on conversations. George eventually came downstairs in the best of spirits and spent the drive home regaling me with stories and family gossip.

I was spending an increasing amount of time on my own writing, beginning to feel a little more confident. In the spring I had written a short story, encouraged not only by George, but also by Alistair Peebles, who edited *the Orkney Arts Review* and who mentioned to me that he planned to run a short story competition to be judged by John Fergusson, senior producer at BBC Radio Orkney. Keith had been out on a fishing boat one morning, taking photographs for *Sea Haven*, and had come to Faravel feeling shaky in the aftermath of seasickness. He lay down to rest for a few hours and while he slept, in the quiet house, I sat at the kitchen table and wrote 'The First Wife' (loosely based, in part, on incidents from my first marriage, transported to an Orkney setting). I have rarely written anything so easily; within a couple of hours it was done. I sent it off, and when the competition results were announced it was declared the winner. I suspect that there were few entries but my delight took no account of that, and George generously shared in my happiness.

Our precious friendship, however, was shifting again on its axis. Over the past few months I had been spending more time with Jim Lawson, at first a colleague and then a friend. He was now becoming more than that, and again there was that slight difficulty and reticence in speaking to George about matters of the heart. Jim lived at 5 Mayburn Court, so he and George already knew one another a little, and when George saw that this relationship was perhaps going to be a serious one he seemed quietly glad for me. Although reluctant to talk about such things, he understood how much I wanted affection and shared domesticity and children, and I hoped that it might be possible to have those things and keep George's friendship too.

November began with two bonfire parties and then a reading by Margaret Elphinstone, who came to stay with me at Faravel. She is known primarily as a novelist but on that occasion she also read from *Outside Eden: The Poetry of Margaret Elphinstone*, and I found her poems inspiring.[27] She came with me to George's and we had a convivial Sunday evening of conversation and drams, and I saw George at Mayburn Court on two other evenings that month. But then I had word that my father was ill, and travelled down to Kent to visit him in hospital; I also made an appointment with my solicitor in London to finalise the sale of my flat, as it was clear that I would never live there again – I was too embedded in Orkney life.

The next few weeks were a deeply unsettling time, full of coming and going. George and I met two days after my trip, but I have no record of seeing him again before I flew back to London to spend Christmas with my parents. I was relieved that my father was out of hospital and recovering well, yet still feeling anxious about him – and about poor Billie, too, who was in the cattery for yet another stay and another bout of fur-pulling – and I was sad because my elderly friend Jessie Mowat had died on the day that I set off on my second journey south. I made sure that I returned in time for her funeral on the 29th, and that evening was spent quietly with Alison Blacklock and George. On the 31st I was setting off yet again, for a few days in Kingussie with Jim. He had lived there for several years before coming to Orkney, and we had a pleasant time visiting his friends. But on 7 January, after the sociable bustle of Hogmanay, I was happy to see George alone at Mayburn Court and catch up with all that had happened in Stromness in my absence.

There were a number of literary events in the first few months of the new year, including a Foy on 22 January – there had been a lot of other social occasions before Christmas, which meant that it was difficult to find a suitable date then, and it was good to have a cheerful evening of this kind to enliven the cold dark days of January. Some of the participants – Pam Beasant, Eddie Cummins and Bessie Grieve – had read before, but there were new local voices too. My nephew Kevin was staying in Orkney for a few days before going to Up Helly Aa, the great annual fire festival in Shetland, and when he arrived at the Pier Arts Centre for the Foy he found that the room was almost bursting at the seams. On 19 March there was a reading by Andrew Greig, who had contacted me some months previously to say that he wanted to visit Orkney. The *Orkney Arts Review* was running another competition, this time for poetry, to be judged by George Gunn, and so, buoyed up by my success with the short story, I submitted several poems with George's encouragement.

There were other, more personal events to arrange too, as Jim and I were to be married quietly in May. Years later, reading George's biography, I discovered that Kenna Crawford also married during the spring of 1991, but George did not mention this to me. He was getting to know Jim better; they both came to Sunday lunch at Faravel at the beginning of February, although my visits to Mayburn Court continued as usual, twice at the end of that month and again at the beginning of March. Jim was at an Open University summer school later in March and I was going to meet him in Cambridge. Margaret Elphinstone arrived the day before I left, to stay at Faravel during my absence. George seemed very pleased when I told him that Jim and I were hoping to buy Tam and Gunnie's house in Ness Road, and while we were away we made several anxious calls to our lawyer to find out how things were progressing. Tam and Gunnie were moving out to the Don, below the Black Craig, where Beverley had lived for many years. George had often enjoyed relaxing in the lovely garden at Ness Road – I remember seeing him there on a sunny Sunday afternoon, waving to me as I walked past on my way to the shore – and it seemed to make him happy to know that he would still be able to sit there sometimes, as well as in the garden at the Don, for which Gunnie had many ambitious plans.

I loved my house at Faravel with its view across to the Orphir hills, but Jim and I both felt that we would like to start afresh in a home that was new to both of us, so I had written to the council asking to end my tenancy and Jim put his house at Mayburn Court up for sale. By mid-April I was starting to pack up my belongings at Faravel and the removal van came for them at the beginning of May; Jim would move his things into the Double Houses after the wedding. I went along to see George twice at Mayburn Court during my first fortnight at Ness Road and it seemed strange not to be coming down the path from Faravel; I was very much aware that this was only one change among many that lay ahead.

The wedding took place in the Church of Scotland in Stromness, early on a Friday evening (following the custom in Orkney), although this was permitted only after an interview at the Manse during which I had to answer questions about my previous marriage and my divorce. We kept it small and quiet: ten people were present, including ourselves: the minister, Reverend Philip Earnshaw; my parents and Jen; Jim's parents and his Aunt Jean; and Alison Blacklock, who was one of the witnesses. After the ceremony, Alistair Peebles took photographs of us in a seafront garden nearby, with the MV *St Sunniva* sailing past in the background, and then we walked a few hundred yards to have a splendid dinner at the Hamnavoe Restaurant. George was not present, although he had been invited. At an early stage I had thoughtlessly asked him if he would care to be one of our witnesses, although if I had been less absorbed in arranging accommodation for my parents, trying to decide on appropriate wedding clothes and trying to fit in the hundred-and-one tasks which moving house entailed, I would have realised that to witness the marriage of a divorced woman might have presented a problem for him. The Saltire Society came to the rescue by deciding that George would be the recipient of the Andrew Fletcher of Saltoun Award (given in recognition of a significant contribution to Scottish culture); the dates of the award ceremony and our wedding clashed, so George duly made his apologies to us, although I can't find a record of whether he did actually go to receive the award.

George's wedding gift to us was an acrostic, mounted and framed by Renée:

> Jousting of rosebuds and wings and waves
> On the pier gardens of Hamnavoe in May
> And there, right on the threshold of summer
> Ness Road – a house that has always had kindness
> and beauty in it
> Number 4 – opens to
> A new-married pair, and we know that the generosity and
> the loveliness will go on.
>
> *
>
> June will shake out roses and butterflies
> In the garden
> Many a summer, we pray, while the dazzling sea dance
> never ceases about the rocks
> and the pier below.

Jim and I went to Papa Westray for a brief honeymoon, and when we returned home our lives did not seem very different at first. Jim was busy with all his usual commitments, but I had passed on my role as literature secretary to Pam Beasant, who made the arrangements when Norman MacCaig came to give a reading in June as the St Magnus Festival poet. I continued to visit George, although less frequently than before, and it was much like old times at Mayburn Court, with evenings spent exchanging the small details of our lives and the lives of others. George told me all about my new neighbour, Nora Wishart (Sylvia Wishart's aunt), recounting stories that she herself didn't feel able to reveal to me for some years until we had an exchange of confidences over a glass of sherry beside her stove one winter afternoon.

I was very happy when George began to spend some evenings with us at Ness Road, although I realised that it must be strange for him to see the house with our things in it instead of Tam and Gunnie's wonderful collection of spongeware, their paintings and antique furniture and beautiful rugs. Nevertheless, he seemed to like coming along, often on a Thursday evening, and to my astonishment he even grew quite friendly with Jim's large and fairly boisterous dog, Gillie, who in spite of his size was a soft-hearted creature and allowed Billie to have the best place in front of the fire. For George's visits I used to buy Stockan's oatcakes and Orkney cheese, and Flett's pork sausages to be eaten cold with a glass or two of Jim's home brew. Sometimes other friends came too, such as Dorrie and Donald Morrison, whose company George enjoyed very much; he and Donald were both wonderful storytellers and could keep us in fits of laughter. Donald told us many tales about life in the Western Isles – he was a Lewis man – and about his numerous Morrison relations. I particularly liked a story about a bus driver who had to ask the passengers for directions because he had forgotten the route. Occasionally the conversation might take a darker turn – Jim remembers his surprise at George's interest in a notorious murder case from the late 1950s. Peter Manuel was a serial killer who murdered at least seven people and was the last person to be hanged in Scotland, and George seemed to know all about it.

My parents travelled up to Orkney in June for their annual visit and George was eager to come along to see them. He and my father found much to talk about, although I think that my mother was rather shy of George. Dorrie and Donald also came to visit my parents; by a strange coincidence, Dorrie and my mother and father had all grown up in the same part of south-east London and they had many reminiscences to share. George occasionally joined us when I took my parents out for a drive, just as he had in the past when they visited me at Faravel. George had his own visitors too, and I was glad to meet Peter and Betty Grant again in July during their stay at Mayburn Court. I saw less of George later that summer, as Jim and I were away in Kingussie and Glasgow at the end of July, and we spent a week at the Bird Observatory on Fair Isle in August.

In spite of all these happy times, my life was becoming difficult again. I began to suffer more frequently from periods of depression and anxiety, and I had several panic attacks at work. I would probably not have been very good company, and gradually George began to slip away from me for a while. I think I hardly noticed this happening until one day someone was telling me about a local event – a book launch or a private view – and mentioned in passing that Surinder Punjya, who had recently moved to Orkney, would be going as George's guest. I felt rather sad as I reflected that at one time I would have been invited to go with George, although I can see now that this change was perhaps as much to do with the fact that I was married to Jim as with Surinder's ascendancy in George's affections. George had been happy to go travelling with Gunnie, but he might have become less inclined to risk any gossip or misunderstanding – not just for himself, but to protect me as well. Even in the early days of our friendship I had been aware of its possible transience – partly because of George's precarious health, and also because in my less self-confident moods I sometimes felt that I had been admitted into a special place where I had no inherent right to be. Looking back, that seems an odd feeling to have had, but I recall it clearly and I think it was a symptom of my rather fragile mental state at the time. Some fragments of never-completed poems reflect this aware-ness of transience: a sense that although I had become part of George's circle for a while, he always belonged essentially to others. Even before this slight estrangement, I had been aware of subtle changes, writing about 'new voices' and a 'conversa-tion that would go on without me', and as my mood darkened it was easy to feel that I was losing my place in George's life.

Nevertheless, Jim and I became good friends with Surinder. I first met him at Mayburn Court and he soon came to visit us at Ness; occasionally I had lunch or tea with him. After a brief stay at a small house in Alfred Street, he rented first a caravan and then a holiday cottage in the grounds of Stenigar, just along the road from us. He also lived for a while in a flat in Stenigar, although I had forgotten this until recently, when I came across one of George's articles, written in 1995, in which he referred to Surinder's 'flat at Stenigar – the "studio flat" they call it, because it was Stanley Cursiter's studio, and has the great window half in the roof and half in the east-facing wall, where Stanley did his painting in the fifties and sixties'.[28] George was often central to my conversations with Surinder, but we also talked about books and writing, for he too was a poet. He and George had quickly developed a strong and lasting bond and I was glad for them both, but I found that I had far less time alone with George now because Surinder was frequently at Mayburn Court when I called. He seemed the least pushy person imaginable, but he did have a quiet persuasiveness

and determination and would not be put off if he felt that
George would benefit from his company or his help. He got
along comfortably with most of George's other friends and was
generally much liked; this was in contrast to what I perceived
as a general antipathy to Renée, whose possessive affection for
George infuriated some of his more long-standing companions.
Ron Ferguson confirms this impression, describing Renée as
George's 'self-appointed gatekeeper' and adding that this 'was
not appreciated by George's friends'.[29]

I was sufficiently troubled about my sense of a new distance
between George and myself to raise the subject with him. In
September I heard only by chance that he was back in hospital
in Aberdeen and this heightened my awareness of how we were
growing apart. I wrote a letter to him – the contents of which I
now only dimly recall – and George's reply began in a soothing
and reassuring tone: 'Thank you very much for your letter. I'm
sure we will be always the best of friends. Of course we haven't
seen much of each other this summer – you and Jim with 4
Ness Road, fitting all your possessions in (which you've done
so beautifully), and I with the summertime visitors mainly.'[30]

But he continued in a way that worried me deeply:

I was quite exhausted in the end, and darkly depressed
– much worse than any previous depression. So ... the
Aberdeen surgeon thought it best for me to be treated at
Foresterhill. So here I've been for the last 5 days, reading a
lot, and drowsing, and writing stuff that's no good just to
keep in practice ...

The treatment seems to be quieting the fevered mind, but
of course it has side effects too. Peter and Betty have been so

kind, visiting me every day, and Betty loaded with goodies
– flowers and fruit and drinks and yoghurt. I haven't let it be
known where I am – because it['s] a strain speaking to too
many visitors. May all be well with you, Jo.

Even in the midst of illness and depression, George could be
generous. He wrote again a few days later when he felt – or
perhaps claimed to feel, to reassure me – a little more hopeful:

I haven't forgotten your birthday. I'm sure it will be a very
happy time for you.

The acrostic will have to be copied on really good paper
– this is just a standby till I get home, whenever that will
be: not too long. The deep depression has eased a bit, not
entirely. But there are gaps in the dark clouds: blue patches
here and there.

This afternoon I'm hoping to go for tea with Peter and
Betty. We might even manage a wee run in the car . . .

I hope to see you soon, Jo . . . Have a lovely birthday.[31]

Tucked in with the letter was 'A Birthday Song':

Just who built those beautiful houses
On the pier at Ness, not
Anyone can say for sure.[32]
Now to know that
Never a kinder person
Assembles birthday friends
about her today, is
sufficient knowledge.

The words 'Never a kinder person' heaped coals of fire on my head. I felt that I had not been kind, or thoughtful; I had not been a particularly good friend to George recently. Yet it seemed that even if I had hurt him, he wanted me to know I had been forgiven.

Life continued to have its ups and downs. Robert Crawford came to give a reading in late September, and my diary records that I saw George several times in October, but I was shaken by the death of Irene Traill Thomson on 13 October; her funeral was held on George's seventieth birthday and I didn't see him that day. The following morning, Jim and I left Orkney to visit his family in Hamilton and then to spend a few days in the Lake District, and it was the end of the month before I had an opportunity to give George his birthday gift, a small embroidered rug.

During this time I was struggling to keep my head above water, and in November, after much indecision and worry, I resigned from my job without another one to go to. It meant that we were suddenly living on one salary instead of two. I doubted that I would get a favourable reference from the school and had little confidence about finding work, and often felt low and exhausted. In December my spirits were lifted by the marvellous news that I was pregnant, but Jim and I decided that we would wait a while before passing this on to our families. We visited my parents in Kent and his in Hamilton over the Christmas holiday, a long and tiring trip, and on 20 January I had a miscarriage. I was thirty-nine years old, and in spite of Dr Rae's attempts to reassure me, I believed that I would never have a child. It was a dark time; I felt locked into a private misery and didn't know how to get out of it – in fact, I hardly knew how to get out of bed in the mornings. Once Jim had left for work I used to take the dog for a walk around the shore, whatever the weather, and in the afternoons I did too much housework, becoming obsessive about dust and the state of the kitchen floor. I had trouble sleeping, and I must have been hell to live with.

I have few recollections of visiting George at that time and he is rarely mentioned in my rather sparse account of the first few months of 1992, although I recorded that he and Surinder came to lunch at Ness Road in late January and that I spent an evening with him in March. I noted that I had been asked to take part in the Foy on 31 January, but not whether George was there to listen, although he featured in the programme: 'No Foy would be complete without the inclusion of the work of George Mackay Brown, and Alison Skene read a refreshingly individual selection . . . moving neatly from a description of Orkney in January to a celebration of the merits of clapshot.'[33]

My diary for that spring shows many appointments at the surgery and interviews at the job centre; I was trying to make a fresh start. 'George's friendship is different – still recovering itself after last summer', I noted in April as I sat in a guest house in Lerwick. I was there alone, needing some time to reflect, and remembering how on my visit to Shetland two years earlier I had felt the healing power of that landscape. I drove for miles on the empty roads and walked along the beautiful coastline; I read and slept. The weather was mostly kind, although as I waited for the airport bus on the last morning there was snow on the ground. I returned to Stromness feeling calmer and less despairing, and before long I was offered a post in Kirkwall as a domestic help at St Rognvald's House, a home for elderly people. I worked in the laundry for a while and then in the kitchen, and cleaned the residents' rooms. I got another job at St Peter's House in Stromness as a relief assistant, helping out when other members of staff were ill or on holiday, and by the summer I had two other part-time jobs as well, as a typist in our lawyer's office and a shop assistant at the Waterfront Gallery. I was exhausted most of the time, but at least I was occupied and contributing to the household finances.

That summer, Jim and I went to France for a holiday. It was by no means an idyllic time, but a photograph taken by friends as we stopped in Kingussie on our way back to Orkney shows us suntanned and smiling. George, however, had been unwell. He had a brief stay in the Balfour Hospital after a cold became something more serious and he found himself 'fighting for breath'.[34] Fortunately, he made a good recovery and by September everything seemed more cheerful, although from the acrostic George gave me for my birthday (I saw him the previous day, on 17 September) it would seem that there were a number of things that he hadn't entirely enjoyed about the summer:

> Journeying to a birthday
> Over touristy summer waves
> A strange voyage it seems sometimes with all that
>   summertime
> Noise and touristy jargoning and pop-din in pubs all the
>   way from
> Ness to Garson.
> And, worst, reek and rowdiness of stampeding wheels.

Look though, swans are over the loch, a lark is up
Against the west.
Warbeth is littered with shells and ox-eyes.
Summer ends now
On a wave of peace and beauty.
Nothing so fitting for a dear friend's birthday.

He was right about the 'wave of peace and beauty': my fortieth
birthday was a calm and memorable day, the sky a very pale
blue with a shimmering haze along the horizon. I spent part
of the morning on the shore at Warebeth – dawdling along
the tideline, throwing driftwood sticks for Gillie – and then
drove to Stenness to see Donella, and we went to the beach
below her house with her youngest son and our dogs. In the
evening, getting ready to go out to dinner with Jim at the
Creel Restaurant in St Margaret's Hope, I felt happy and
hopeful, and within a few weeks I knew that I was pregnant
again.

My diary gives a patchy account of the following months,
and George's name appears only sporadically. I gave up my
job at St Peter's House in the autumn but was still working
part-time for the lawyer's office and at the Waterfront Gallery,
and going to evening classes at the Academy, sometimes
calling in to see George on my way home. I saw him briefly
at Mayburn Court on his birthday and we met again at the
end of October. Edwin Morgan was in Orkney that month to
give a reading, but I didn't note whether or not George was
there, or at the winter Foy in December when I was among
the participants. I was spending quite a lot of time at Rae's
Close with Granny, who had celebrated her ninety-second

birthday in July, and one of the last entries for 1992 was written on 9 December after I had been to see her: 'Eclipse of the moon . . . standing on the pier with my black coat over my nightdress, watching the eclipse begin – Surinder & Jim coming past.'

4

A BIRTH AND A DEATH

A mystery abides. We move from silence into silence, and
there is a brief stir between, every person's attempt to make a
meaning of life and time.[1]

George Mackay Brown

In the notebook for 1993 in which I kept a record of thoughts
and feelings, rather than merely the dates of appointments and
events, there is one brief entry on 26 January and then a blank
until 14 May: 'And I've written nothing . . . Four months of
what has perhaps been one of the happiest times of my life.
The attention; the fuss; the sudden camaraderie . . . There have
been downs, of course . . . exhaustion and discomfort.' During
the first few months of the year, I had settled into routines that
would be well and truly broken for me in June, when I was due
to give birth; in my engagement diary there are brief reminders
of visits to George, often on Tuesday or Thursday evenings, or
Saturday afternoons, and cups of tea with Dorrie and Donald
and Granny. I enjoyed going to a reading by Ron Butlin in
February and one by Bernard MacLaverty in March, thankful

in some ways that it was no longer my responsibility to organise such events. In April I wrote 'Valerie's 3-ish + GMB', which perhaps meant a visit to Valerie Brajuha in Finstown but I have no memory of it. But between the dates of these outings are notes of a different kind: 'Got triple blood test results'; 'Felt baby move'; 'Midwife came.' Antenatal classes began, and the surgery staff booked a flight for me to Aberdeen; I was such an 'elderly' primigravida at the age of forty that I had little choice about being sent to the mainland two weeks before the birth, to minimise any risk.

At Aberdeen Maternity Hospital there was accommodation for island-dwelling women and their visiting husbands or partners, and their other children. In spite of having dreaded this incarceration, I enjoyed it: I made friends with Meg from Hoy and Kathy from Shetland; sometimes we cooked meals together in the shared kitchen. During the day we caught the bus into town, or wandered around the Botanic Gardens and sat eating cake in the café. In the evenings we occasionally went to the pub across the road for non-alcoholic drinks, and what a sight we must have been – three whale-like women, all within two weeks of giving birth. I noted on 29 May that fog had descended over the city and on 1 June I wrote just one word: '*Tired.*' Kathy's father came to visit her, then Meg's partner arrived, and Jim flew down from Orkney on 4 June to keep me company for the last few days.

I wrote to tell George about my adventures, and in his reply he regaled me with all that I was missing back home:

Thinking about you a lot these days . . .
I phoned Jim one evening and he said you're feeling OK.

146

I'll phone him again this weekend. It is good of you to write in this busy exciting time for you, Jo.

(I forgot Jim will be with you now. I'm sure that's good for you both, and no doubt for the little stranger who's about to make his/her eagerly-looked-forward-to bow.)

I hope you 3 fruitful ladies from the north had a good drink in the pub . . .

The Folk Festival went over like a wave (of lager whisky & song) last weekend. I stayed at home. The St Magnus Festival in a fortnight: I'll have to sally out on 2 or 3 occasions. (There are 2 lavish buffets: Highland Park and ELF – on the same day unfortunately). Now a 3rd buffet invitation has come by post!

My mother's birthday was yesterday, so I wrote a poem about her: too early to know whether it's good or not . . .

Renée's London family have left now . . . her grandson, wife, & 5-year-old son . . .

Surinder has quite recovered. Mrs Moyle his neighbour [in Coventry, where his family lived] has sent *yet another* pullover, colour mustard or old gold. Plus a banana cake. The cake you gave me was delicious, Jo: and I really enjoyed the mince. I hope that next week brings the good news.

Much love meantime from George.[2]

The poem about George's mother was a moving history of her origins in Sutherland, her marriage and her life in Stromness, and included these lines:

> Gentleness, poverty, six children
> (One died) in stone houses
> Along Hamnavoe, at close and pier.

A cupboard sparse but never empty,
Oatcakes and bannocks on a smoking griddle,
The Monday washing
Flaunting, damp flags, in a walled garden,

The paraffin lamp on the winter table,

Jar of bluebells on a sun-touched sill,

And a wordless song moving
    Through the house, upstairs, downstairs,
[. . .]
Today, June the fourth, 1993
Mhari – her death month November –
Had been one hundred and two.[3]

In the meantime, I was waddling around Aberdeen in the last stages of pregnancy, with an aching back, and feet swollen by the heat. Jim and I went out to dinner in the evenings, wondering when our child would make its appearance; waiters would kindly ask when the baby was due and look alarmed when we told them that it could be any time now. Nothing happened on the appointed day, but Emma was born in the early hours of 11 June and the news duly reached George, who wrote on 13 June:

Now we all hope to see you and the little daughter in Stromness very soon, with all a lovely summer in front of you.

    I won't tire you with too long a letter but just to let you know how pleased we all are. Renée visited last night, and

was delighted ... Next thing to learn is the baby's name.
Blessings on you both, and Jim too.[4]

Both sets of grandparents came up to Orkney in July to meet
their new grandchild, but what should have been a happy
time was shadowed by worries about my health. Shortly after
Emma's birth I experienced intense pain in my left side, and
Emma and I were readmitted to the Balfour Hospital. A scan
revealed a large ovarian tumour, but it wasn't possible for me
to have the operation I needed in Orkney and so just after my
birthday in September we flew back to Aberdeen. The previous
week, George had written me yet another poem:

> Just one person there was to greet
> On birthdays four or five Septembers ago
> At Faravel.
> Next, at Ness Road, there were two round the cake and
>   candles.
> Now, a new dweller under that rooftree,
> And this and all birthdays to come enriched by Emma's
>   presence!

I wondered, as the plane took off and the islands fell away below,
just how many birthdays I might have left. As I was still feeding
Emma myself, my GP had made arrangements for her to come
to Aberdeen with me, and although many of the nurses coped
brilliantly with this inconvenience, the ward sister did not. After
the operation I was at my wits' end, trying to feed and change
Emma and lift her in and out of a high-sided hospital cot while
still feeling sore and stiff. The hospital chaplains and other

patients rescued me with kindness; someone found a pram and walked Emma along the hospital corridors; an Orkney friend in the maternity hospital visited me; someone I had never met before brought flowers from her garden. I tried to keep cheerful but was privately terrified of what the future might hold for Emma if my tumour proved to be malignant. Fortunately that was not the case, and two weeks later I was back at home again, more or less in one piece.

At some point after Emma's birth, George brought a poem he had written for her, 'A New Child: ECL – 11 June 1993'. With all that had been happening, I stopped keeping a diary for a while and so the precise date is lost, but I remember that he asked whether I would be happy for it to be published. He subsequently decided to revise it a little and the new version eventually appeared in *Following a Lark*,[5] a collection in which Maggie Fergusson detects 'a powerful nostalgia for infancy'.[6] George gave me a handwritten copy, the words slanting across the page in his inimitable writing, and we put it in a frame and hung it in Emma's room, where it still is at the time of writing. When George revised the poem he omitted the lines 'There are "cats" on the pier / There are "gulls", "fish" ' from the end of the third stanza, and added a word to the fourth stanza: '*All* scored on the chart'. The final stanzas are quite different in the original:

I   Wait awhile, small voyager
              On the shore, with seapinks and shells

        The boat
              Will take a few summers to build
        That you must make your voyage in

II   You will learn the names.
That golden light is "sun", "moon"
    The silver light
That grows and dwindles.
And the beautiful small splinters
    That wet the stones, "rain"

III   There is a voyage to make,
    A chart to read,
But not yet, not yet.
        "Daisies" spill from your fingers.
    The night daisies are "stars"
There are "cats" on the pier.
    There are "gulls"; "fish"

IV   The keel is laid, the strakes
    Will be set, in time.
    A tree is growing
    That will be a tall mast

All about you, meantime
The music of humanity,
    The dance of creation:
All scored on the chart of the voyage

V   Listen long to stories and songs
    of other islands, ports, people
Till your ship is ready
The voyage of Emma to Tir-Nan-Og
You will not miss that landfall

VI   May St Magnus be on the shore with you
               At the time of crabs and sillocks,
               At the time of mid-sea waves,
               The horizon music,
               And at the helm, a shining friend,
               with you

VII   And may The Star of The Sea
               shine on your voyage.

My relationship with George was gradually settling down again; it felt almost like the happiest companionship of earlier times. I walked along to see him on fine evenings, with Emma tucked into a pouch against my chest, and he seemed to like these visits. Surinder was often there too and they both made a great fuss of me and treated Emma as if she were a princess. The intermittent entries in my diary for the latter part of that year consist chiefly of notes about Emma's latest achievements – of little account to anyone else, but thrilling to her proud parents: 'Smiled at self and me in mirror'; 'Smiled when she caught sight of Jim'; 'Playing with beakers; good control, lifting blue one to mouth'; 'Strong attempt to crawl.'

    I'm afraid that I must endlessly have related all these things to George, who was nevertheless always patient and gave a good impression of being interested. At Christmas, one of my gifts was *A Mother's Journal* and in this volume my notes on childhood landmarks such as Emma's first steps and her early vocabulary are interspersed with events of wider significance: '25 January. We met Peter Maxwell Davies, who greeted us like old friends. He has just finished his Fifth Symphony. Dorrie was out but we had coffee with Surinder'. (The premiere of Symphony No. 5 was at the Royal Albert Hall in London, on 9 August.) I mentioned a long walk over Brinkie's Brae with Emma in the pushchair and then added: 'Emma visited George Mackay Brown in the evening (Archie, Elizabeth and Aimée Bevan were there too). She stared at Archie and beamed at Aimée' (who was one of Archie and Elizabeth's granddaughters). There was a New Year's Foy on 21 January, when George's great-nephew Magnus Dixon and I were amongst those taking part, and Duncan McLean's review praised Magnus's story for showing 'maturity beyond his 17 years', adding that ' "The Bay" shows great promise. More than promise; it was enjoyed by a rapt audience.'[7]

In February I took Emma to see George one afternoon before we went to visit Granny at Rae's Close, and Gypsy was there because George was looking after her for three weeks. He wrote in 'Under Brinkie's Brae' about anticipating Gypsy's return to Deerness with some sadness: 'There will be nobody to greet me in the morning, with cat-songs, as soon as I open the bedroom door. Nobody to eat bits of cheese or fish from my fingers (for she likes to eat in company, rather than just off the kitchen floor). Nobody to boss me around, silently.'[8] Later that month I noted that Emma was getting good at remembering and pronouncing names, 'Lorna & George & Josh', although there were other less successful attempts, such as 'Baddie and Updie' for our friends Debbie and Timothy, and 'Zozo' for Mr Cecil Steer.

One day in March I went out early to buy bread and fish for George and Surinder, who were staying at the Don while Tam and Gunnie were away, and parked in a lay-by near the Standing Stones of Stenness, 'listening to Clannad, watching the stones & the sky & the next storm coming. Then the Don, & soup with Surinder & George – a beautiful room – Gunnie's lovely things.' It felt strange to be in the house that had once been Beverley's home; it was considerably changed now, a dividing wall having been demolished to make a larger space. Emma and I went to see George and Surinder again, to invite them to her christening on Sunday the 27th, when Jim's parents were visiting from the mainland. I spent days baking for the christening tea, and there was so much left over that I took a selection of cakes round to Mayburn Court afterwards, as George was back in his own house by then. On the 30th, George and Surinder came along to Ness for the evening and drank home brew, to celebrate the end of Jim's school term, while storm-force winds raged outside, and two days later, on Good Friday, we had several visitors at Ness in the afternoon, including 'George (with a chocolate duck for E.) & Surinder'. All these occasions were a source of great happiness for me, as I realised that it was still possible to be part of George's life, and as I saw his pleasure in being with Emma.

The *Mother's Journal* records many other visits and outings. In April I took Emma and George out to lunch; we tried the Merkister Hotel first, a favourite place of mine beside the Harray Loch, but they weren't serving lunches that day and so we went instead to the Standing Stones Hotel, where 'Emma sat in a highchair & ate half of GMB's strawberry ice cream'. At the beginning of May I drove Emma and George to Warebeth beach in the afternoon, 'a glorious warm blue day – like summer'. If George was coming to Ness for beer and sausages we used to let Emma stay up a little later, which was hardly difficult as she rarely wanted to sleep in the evenings.

A slightly blurred photograph captures one such occasion, also in May: George is sitting on the sofa next to Emma, teasing her and laughing. My parents were staying at Stenigar, where they could sleep peacefully without being woken in the early hours by our lively daughter, and a picture taken by my mother on the 14th shows George with a glass of beer in his hand, gazing at Emma as she stands supported by my hands. I noted that 'GMB came to dinner (which was a bit noisy) & Dorrie & Donald came later for drinks. Emma wouldn't settle & stayed up until 10.30, laughing & enjoying herself.' George sang 'On the Good Ship Lollipop' to her, and made the most wonderfully realistic miaowing noises that delighted and confused her because she couldn't see any cats in the room – dear Billie had died shortly after Emma's birth.

After my parents left I suddenly felt tired and low. My father was almost eighty years old, my mother five years younger, and I felt sad that they would share so little of Emma's childhood. My mother often said that she was happy for us to be in Orkney because she knew that we were safe there, but I fretted about being so far away. I drove to Warebeth one evening after Emma was asleep, needing to be alone: 'Nets burning on the shore. Incredible light. Hills of Caithness visible.' I lay awake almost all that night, but in the morning my mood lifted and I felt able to face the challenges of the coming weeks. Emma was a beautiful, loving and intelligent baby, but her first year was not without its worries: Jim's mother had noticed during her visit in March that Emma was having difficulty in focusing on objects close to her, and we had somehow failed to observe this. It meant a series of appointments with an orthoptist at the Balfour Hospital, and at the age of only ten months Emma had to wear the smallest pair of glasses imaginable. George thought they were delightful and mentioned them in her first birthday acrostic in June:

Emma Catherine
May you have a happy first birthday.
My goodness, is that Gillie barking
A happy birthday to you, dear Emma?

Can't you hear the seagulls
At the end of the pier, crying
'This is Emma's birthday, hoorah!'
Harken, the little pussy-cats of the South
End are gossiping:
'Right enough, I heard that too.
It's Emma Lawson's birthday . . .'
Now the blackbird in the garden breaks into thrilling
    song,
'Emma, you beautiful child, many happy returns!'
*

Oh, and what friends will be arriving at
Ness Road, with cards and greetings and gifts!
Emma will twinkle through her spectacles, at the centre of the
chorussing circle of animals and
birds and children.

Later that month, Seamus Heaney came to give a reading during the St Magnus Festival, and a photograph was taken in the Stromness Hotel of him and George sitting together, 'with cups of cold coffee on the table before us – the coffee was there purely for design and atmosphere – and the pleasant young photographer Ian takes a clutch of pictures for *The Independent*.[9] Although I did not know it at the time, on midsummer night George was wandering outside our house, enjoying the 'magnificent' light: 'I took a late stroll along Ness Road and spoke to a small shrill-voiced black and white cat on the wall at "Ruah", and walked round the Double Houses and came home to have a poached egg on toast. The last of the sun was just leaving the Mayburn balcony.'[10]

Moira Burgess visited Orkney again in July, not for a reading but to bring her children for a holiday. They rented 80 Victoria Street, a small house on Clouston's Pier just off the main street in Stromness, without realising that it was the place where George had been born. 'I had no idea of this', Moira wrote to me, 'but it emerged in conversation and he said he'd never been back there since he was five.'[11] She suggested that he should go along to see what the house was like, although she didn't really expect him to turn up. 'But one afternoon there came a knock at the door. He wrote it all up in the *Orcadian* . . . so I need say no more, except how delighted I was to be able to do this for him.' Sure enough, in 'Under Brinkie's Brae' he described that afternoon:

My first memories are of a house – 80 Victoria Street – half on the street and half down Clouston's pier. There I sat on the doorstep . . . in early childhood, watching the town go by . . .

We left Victoria Street in 1926 or '27, just after I had started at the infant school, and moved to 3 Melvin Place, in the vicinity of the Public Library in Hellihole Road.

THE SEED BENEATH THE SNOW

And from that day until yesterday, I had never been inside 80 Victoria Street.

A Glasgow novelist, Moira Burgess, spends many of her summer holidays in Stromness. Talking to each other the other Sunday evening, Moira told me she had rented 80 Victoria Street for two weeks, with her son and daughter.

She agreed to show me the old place.

Everybody is interested in the place of their first beginning, as the salmon seeks its native stream.[12]

George went on to compare his recollections of the house with its modernised interior and gave a moving account of what he thought was his earliest memory: 'my father silhouetted against that very window, reading a letter . . . I was sitting up in a pram watching him.' He had already recorded that precious moment in his autobiography: 'Early years are remembered in gleams only, and the gleams illumine what seem to be quite unimportant incidents. I remember sitting up in a pram, aged maybe two or three, and watching the silhouette of my father, in his postman's hat, against the window; he seemed to be reading a sheet of paper.'[13] When George wrote to Moira at the end of that month, he began by thanking her 'for letting me see my birth-house' and added 'I wonder if my mother would have recognized it?'

Moira came to see us at Ness Road on the afternoon of 8 July, although it was probably not an entirely pleasant visit for her: the *Mother's Journal* reveals that Jim and I were supposed to go to a wedding party that night, but 'Emma had a dreadful day of teeth and cold so we rang Freya (our babysitter) and cancelled. We were exhausted.'

We set off on our own holiday a few days later, travelling
through Scotland and as far as Kent to visit our families and
friends and staying away for several weeks. George mentioned
to Moira that I was missing Orkney's climate: 'A letter from
Joanna in London; sizzling in the heat. "Oh for a breath of
Atlantic wind!" she says . . . They return tomorrow.'[14] He also
told Moira that my mother's dog had bitten me because it
was jealous of Emma, and no doubt this incident confirmed
George's general prejudice against dogs, but although the dog
may indeed have been jealous, the more obvious reason for the
nip was that it had dozed off against my foot under the dining
table and been startled when I moved. George ended his letter
to Moira by saying: 'The sun is trying hard to break through
the webs of haar.' He seemed preoccupied with the weather,
writing in 'Under Brinkie's Brae' about the contrast between
Orkney and the south: 'We keep talking about the weather to
everybody. "Yes, what a lovely summer!" . . . "Yes, aren't we
lucky, compared to the people in the south of England, sizzling
in ninety degrees!" . . . "The lovely fresh airs off the sea".'[15] I was
never very good at coping with high temperatures and looked
forward to September, when George wrote a 'Birthday Ode'
for me:

> Just when the summer leaves are crisping
> On the Double Houses tree
> And Gillie
> Now thinks of buying himself a winter coat and
> Now, also, Emma
> Arranges beautiful phrases on the harp of her mouth;

Lamps are lit earlier, night
After night, and
Whiter the stars cluster, the moon is a
Silver plate; now
On the threshold of the equinox,
Now, surely, today, we ought to celebrate a birthday.

Alistair Peebles contacted me during the autumn to ask if I would write something about George for the *Orkney Arts Review*, as his novel *Beside the Ocean of Time* had been shortlisted for the Booker Prize.[16] George was already being besieged by journalists and I didn't want to add to the pressure, but he kindly agreed to let me interview him and offered to write down his responses to anything else I wanted to know. 'I've given answers of a sort', he wrote in pencil in a note attached to the sheet of questions I gave him after we spent a pleasant evening together, 'not terribly illuminating, but maybe Alistair can use them. It's you who have the hard work of stitching it all together. I enjoyed myself very much last night. The questions are of less moment than Emma.' He said that if he won the prize he believed it would make no difference to his life or to his work; he lived very simply and did not need the money. Although he avoided saying so, he clearly had no intention of going south for the occasion. The attention and excitement were all too much for him; Maggie Fergusson comments that Surinder was away during this time (his father was dying) and that 'George desperately missed his support, both practical and moral.'[17]

George had other close friends, however, such as the Bevans and the Murrays, and his family too, and they helped him through this rather traumatic period. I managed to thread George's thoughts about the Booker into an article that appeared in the *Orkney Arts Review*,[18] and he was also interviewed by two pupils from the Academy, 'for the school magazine. Having once been a schoolboy myself at Stromness Academy, I could hardly deny them. But I fervently hope that Finn Aberdein and Darren Johnstone will ask me simple civil questions ... They did.'[19] Although George disliked being interviewed – he felt like a 'poor fish ... squirming on the hook'[20] – he could be kind and patient about it, as he was when answering my questions about the Booker prize.

Jenny Noble, the daughter of friends of Jim's in Kingussie, came to visit Orkney for a holiday and told us that she was writing a piece about George's work for her Certificate of Sixth Year Studies (she later went on to do further research on George when she was at university in Glasgow, writing a dissertation on George and Edwin Muir).[21] She asked us if there was any chance that we might arrange a meeting with George and he agreed to this without hesitation, so I took her down to Mayburn Court one evening and she was greeted with warmth and friendliness. After the introductions and a cup of tea I left them to their conversation, and Jenny told us afterwards that George had been thoughtful and helpful. Moira Burgess remembers a similar occasion, when she and her children called in to see George on their way to a favourite spot on the West Shore, and found that he already had a visitor – a young student from the University of St Andrews, who was attempting to interview him for a dissertation. 'It wasn't going swimmingly – as you can probably imagine', Moira wrote to me, 'and when we arrived George dashed off to make a cup of tea, with some relief I felt.' Moira chatted to the student and mentioned to him that her niece, Mhairi, had been at St Andrews but was taking a year

---

THE SEED BENEATH THE SNOW

out to have a baby, and it turned out that the student was a friend of the niece and her partner: 'When George reappeared with the tea I said "George, you'll never guess, Alistair knows my niece – ". He was delighted, and I heard later from Mhairi that once we'd gone, the ice had been broken and the boy got a wonderful interview.'[22]

I saw George less frequently during that winter, as much of his time was spent in the company of Surinder and Renée. Surinder devoted himself to George, doing his shopping, posting letters and collecting his prescriptions and his pension for him, and I think he would have waited on him hand and foot if George had allowed it. The only adverse effect of all this kindness was that it meant that George had fewer reasons to go out, even on a pleasant day, and he kept to the house more than he might otherwise have done. But sometimes he did venture along to Surinder's cottage, and from my living-room window I would see him making his way slowly along Ness Road, pausing every so often to rest and to look at the view.

From the turn of the year, however, George's name crops up more often and it is clear that Emma was beginning to get to know him better and to respond to him. The *Mother's Journal* entry for 25 January 1995 records that 'GMB came in the evening & played with her & sang to her. Before he arrived she said "George".' He wisely stayed indoors for a day or two when the weather became cold and icy: 'frosty days, with saltings of new snow over the shiny patches . . . One morning last week, Brian Murray warned me not to set foot on the Mayburn balcony: it was a solid sheet of ice.' Renée (who celebrated her ninety-fourth birthday on 5 February) lent George a walking stick to get safely down the brae after their lunch together at

Quildon Cottage and it was a great help: 'I haven't ventured out since without it.'[23]

He came with Surinder to see us at Ness on the evening of 24 February and again on 22 March, and then he and Surinder went to stay at the Don for a short holiday. I was happy to read George's words in 'Under Brinkie's Brae': 'One of the joys of living is to discover a new writer of genius. (When I say "new", I mean new to me; this writer died in 1952, aged ninety-two.)'[24] He was referring to the Norwegian author Knut Hamsun, whose books he had found at Tam and Gunnie's; he explained that he and Surinder were looking after 'a dog and a cat at the beautiful cottage of Don in Outertown'. Some of his regular readers might have been surprised to learn that George was caring for a dog, as his dislike of them was well known, but he made an exception for Nuff and always had a kind word and a pat for Gillie when he came to Ness. But the important thing for me was that he was still experiencing 'the joys of living'.

At Easter we received a gift from George – *The Wreck of the Archangel*, inscribed 'To Jo, Jim and Emma from George' – but his name rarely appears in my journal during April. In 'Under Brinkie's Brae' in May he admitted that he had been suffering from 'a mild wakeful depression' and quoted Hopkins: 'What hours, O what black hours we have spent / This night!' He also mentioned his sorrow at the death of dear Gypsy – 'I think I have been too sad, up to now, to report the death of Gypsy, the famous cat, at the age of eighteen.'[25] One lovely, happy event in May, however, was at Woodwick House in Evie. Jim, Emma and I were invited to the private view of an exhibition of sculpture by Helen Denerley in collaboration with the painters Simon Fraser, Pat Semple and Peter Goodfellow, and also with George. The exhibition was titled *Beauty and the Beast* and the accompanying leaflet invited the visitor to 'explore parts of the house, the bluebell woodland and the garden, the burn, the grotto and the doocot [dovecot] and discover 60 creations and a pool of poetry'.

George's contributions consisted of phrases to accompany the sculptures, and 'Inscriptions for Garden Bowls'. It's difficult to convey the extraordinary beauty and impact of this exhibition, first viewed on a bright evening when the house and garden were full of sunlight. To see George's words used in this way was profoundly moving: 'Wait for the hour / When dust is blossom and birdsong' read one inscription; another was 'We rise, flowers / On tall ladders of dew and light'. For a sculpture of doves, George composed this: 'We are folded here / Through stormy rainbows / On the ark's rigging'; and for the lizards he wrote: 'Stranger in cold Orkney / We flicker, cold flames / At the corner of sea-folks' eyes'. Wandering happily around that sunny garden, I had no presentiment that in less than a year George would no longer be amongst us.

We celebrated Emma's second birthday in June. There was a cold north wind and a grey sky, but it was a happy day nonetheless. Pam Beasant came with her children for tea and cake, and Surinder called in for a while. In the *Mother's Journal* I mentioned that 'George came when she was in her bath, & stayed until her bedtime', and I have a vivid memory of that evening. I had suggested to George that he might like to wander along and share the birthday cake with us, but he hadn't appeared during the afternoon and I guessed he must be tired after going up to Quildon Cottage for lunch with Renée. Jim went out in the evening and I was alone in the house with Emma, bathing her in her bedroom, as our so-called bathroom had a shower but not a bath. Consequently, her bedtime routine involved a rather precarious arrangement with a baby-bath on a plastic sheet on her bedroom floor, and on more than one occasion her antics tipped the bath. I heard a knock at the door but couldn't leave Emma alone, so I opened the sash window as far as it would go and peered out at George standing below.

'Oh Jo!' I remember him calling up to me, 'Am I too late?' The front door was always unlocked in those days, so he came in and I heard his slow tread on the stairs. He explained that an unexpected visitor had come in the afternoon, preventing him from going out, but here he was at last, glad to see Emma before she went to sleep. He sat in the armchair in her room, watching and chatting to us as I knelt on the floor drying her and playing with her and getting her ready for bed. There seemed to be a special closeness between us that evening, and I have often recalled that peaceful, precious hour. When George left, he gave me an envelope containing Emma's birthday poem:

Emma, now you're two
May you have
Many a happy summer day
Among the Ness Road flowers and butterflies and birds.

Let your feet twinkle on sunny
Afternoons among Warbeth
Waves and rockpools.
Soon, you'll give names to sillocks, cornstalks, stars,
On the long happy road to the Land-of-Three.
Now, however, today, two candles – small pillars of
    purity – on a beautiful cake!

Emma had an appointment at the eye clinic on the day after her birthday, and Surinder came with us for moral support. He called at Ness Road the following day to say goodbye, as he was going away for a while, and I noted that Emma tried out some of her latest words on him: 'yes please', 'hug', 'tissue paper' and 'oatcake'. My parents arrived on 19 June and we were busy with outings to Corrigall Farm Museum and the waterfall in the grounds of Woodwick House, and they were able to see the exhibition too, but there is no mention in my journal of whether we saw George at all during their visit.

Jim, Emma and I went across to the mainland early in July and were away for three weeks, visiting friends and relations in Scotland and England, but, in a letter to Moira Burgess, George said that he hoped to have the company of Peter and Betty Grant at the end of that month: 'They missed last year, first summer in 30 years: both being unwell. But now things are better. Alan graduated a few days ago'. He summed up the first part of his year, which had been 'quite productive . . . I've written a few stories and poems, apart from many poems to illustrate Gunnie Moberg's book of photographs due out next June. They (Murray) are bringing out a book of my stories at the end of summer.' He added, with regard to Moira's own writing, 'it can't be as easy in a big city as in quiet green islands'.[26]

I have few memories or written accounts of seeing George during the later part of that year – the journal pages are mostly blank – but he wrote another acrostic for my birthday in September, including some delightful suggestions as to how I might occupy myself in the future:

Joanna, have a happy day
On your birthday, with Jim and Emma
And your good friends.
No time, these 2½ years, for reading many books.
No, but you could write (for example)
Adventures of Emma, followed by

Little Emma in London
And then *Early Songs and Sayings of Emma*,
Walks through Stromness with Emma and Gillie, followed by
Sunlight and Flowers and Butterflies in Emma's Garden.
Oh no, little time for reading books, but
Now, on this special day, here's one small birthday verse.

I took George out to lunch on the day after his own birthday, having spent an evening with him at Mayburn Court during the previous week, but then his name is absent from my journal until the end of the year, although Fiona Shaw's remarkable rendering of T. S. Eliot's poem *The Wasteland* was shown on television on 23 December and I remember that George and I discussed her mesmerising performance, which we watched together. A notebook containing lists of Christmas presents given and received reminds me that I made biscuits for George and that his gift to Emma was a book about the Nativity.

The New Year came in quietly. George visited us at Ness Road on the evening of 4 January 1996 and there was a New Year's Foy at the end of the month, at which I had been asked to read, but I didn't record whether George came to it. A diary entry on 4 February says simply 'See George', with a cross after it, and on the 9th I wrote 'George's', with no other details.

I must have seen him, because the piece I wrote for the *Hoy Sound*, quoted earlier, describes getting shopping for him on an icy January day, but there is no mention of any evenings spent together. On 12 February I reminded myself to 'Invite George this week' and his name appears with a question mark after it on the 26th, but on 4 March I wrote 'See George this week' and underlined it, suggesting that I still hadn't managed to arrange an evening with him, although I did eventually see him, with Surinder, on 22 March. He might have been happily occupied with visits from other friends and relations, but my engagement diary is so full of playgroup meetings, coffee mornings and doctor's appointments that it's hard not to be troubled by regrets – for the time I didn't give, the things I didn't do, the feelings I didn't express.

That spring, a bright object appeared in the sky, passing close to the earth, trailing a tail of gas and dust. This was the comet Hyakutake, visible from Stromness even above the glow of the street lamps. It must have seemed even brighter from the darkness of Outertown, where George was staying at that time. Surinder had invited him to spend a week or two at Leagar, as he was looking after the house while Matilda and Christopher and their sons were away. Everyone seemed to think that a brief holiday would be good for George, especially since he usually enjoyed such sojourns in the countryside: he always seemed pleased to be asked to stay at the Don, with its view across to the Kame of Hoy. It has been claimed that George was longing for a change of scene,[27] but when he talked to me about the Leagar plan he seemed rather reluctant, wondering aloud if he would sleep well in a strange bed. Despite this, the visit went ahead. I rang after a couple of days to speak to him; he said he had a slight cold and that he and Surinder were finding themselves unequal to keeping the stove alight. He mentioned that he wasn't sleeping well, just as he had feared, and that he felt out of sorts, joking rather darkly that he blamed 'that maleficent comet'. The conversation stayed in my mind because 'maleficent' was a new word to me and I had to look it up.

It was the last conversation that we ever had, because the next time I rang, George was resting and didn't come to the telephone. Surinder explained that George's cold was worse and advised me not to visit, as it might be tiring for him, and in subsequent calls the news was much the same: George was tired and unwell and was best left to recover quietly. I tried not to fret too much, acknowledging that he had suffered from colds before and got over them, although occasionally there had been problems with his breathing. I remembered that at least once he had needed to go to the Balfour Hospital to be given oxygen. I told myself that I must not fuss, that soon George would be safely back at Mayburn Court where I would be able to see him and talk to him again. Had I known it, there was, in fact, a stream of visitors arriving at Leagar, more determined than I was. A doctor attended him; Renée went with supplies of food; someone else took out an electric heater; other friends delivered herbal potions for his cold.

For a long time after George died I tormented myself with pointless questions: why had I not insisted on seeing George? If I had done so, would it have made any difference? Of course not, although we might have had one last conversation face to face – yet without knowing that it would be the last. Had George perhaps said that he wanted to see certain visitors but not others? This seemed possible. Still haunted by that maleficent comet, I allowed my imagination to run riot. Had George believed that it foretold his death? I visualised him lying in a bed that was not his own, watching the sky through drawn-back curtains, searching for the comet's sinister glow.

The end came very quickly. On Friday 12 April, Surinder rang to tell me that George had been taken into the Balfour – just so that they could keep an eye on him, he said. Both Maggie Fergusson and Ron Ferguson refer to Derrick Johnstone, who drove George into Kirkwall that day, as George's GP, but he had retired from the Stromness practice several years earlier.[28] If he made the decision to take George into hospital, it was as his friend rather than his doctor. It was agreed that I would give Surinder a lift into Kirkwall on Saturday afternoon so that we could visit George together. It was Katrina Bevan's second birthday – she is one of Archie and Elizabeth's grandchildren – and on the Saturday morning there was a small party at Hopedale, to which Jim, Emma and I were all invited. It was a sunny morning and a pleasant gathering, and although the day was slightly shadowed by my concern about George, my predominant feeling was one of relief that I was going to see him that afternoon.

After lunch, Surinder, Emma and I set off in the car. As we turned into the Balfour car park, I saw George's brother, Jackie Brown, walking slowly through the entrance. Then I saw Allison and Fraser Dixon going in at a quicker pace, followed by a number of other people who all had some family connection to George. My heart sank as I realised that something must be seriously wrong, and I gathered Emma up in my arms, shaking slightly, dreading to think what we would find. Allison Dixon took me aside in the hospital corridor and told me, as gently as she could, that George was dying; I think she was one of the few people who understood how much I cared for him. She urged me to go in to see him, but the room was quite small and it seemed to be full of people, most of them members of George's family. I hesitated, and yet I wanted so much to be able to say goodbye. I was still holding Emma, who caught sight of the figure lying in the bed and exclaimed: 'That isn't George! His head is all round.' I understood what she meant: George's hair, normally rather thick and springy, was damp and combed flat across his head, so that he looked quite different.

Allison took Emma from me and gently pushed me forward towards George's bed. A nurse told me that I should speak to him because he might be able to hear me, although he seemed to be unconscious. George's brother was sitting at the other side of the bed, and as I moved forward and took hold of George's hand which lay lifelessly on the bedcover, Jackie looked up at me with some surprise, asking me who I was – we had met only once or twice. I gave him my name and said that I was a friend of George's, and then I spoke to George somewhat incoherently, telling him that I was so sorry to see him like this; that we all wanted him to get well; that we all cared so much for him. His eyes were closed and there was no response.

After a little while I let go of his hand and left his bedside, and from that point my recollections are confused, although there are a few moments of clarity: I spoke to Allison Dixon again in the corridor, thanking her for looking after Emma and for giving me those last few moments with George. I went outside, walking slowly, reluctant to leave, as if by staying I could stave off something irrevocable, something dreadful. I rang Jim to explain what was happening, and then I must have

put Emma in her car seat, driven with Surinder to the supermarket, chosen the things we needed, queued up and paid for
them, but I have no recollection of any of that; the next thing I
remember is standing in the car park, putting bags of shopping
into the boot – somehow, ridiculously, there was a need to go
on as if everything was normal, as if George were not going to
die. Someone I knew went past and shouted out a greeting,
asking how I was. I blurted out that George was dying and I
remember the look of shock registering on a face, without being
able to recall now whose face it was. All around me, people were
packing their weekend shopping into their cars, coming and
going with trolleys across the grey tarmac. I felt dread and fear,
as if the world was ending. Those few moments in the car park
amount to one of my clearest memories of the day of George's
death.

Perhaps I should have been telling myself that George was a
frail and elderly man. Given the precarious state of his health
during recent years, I should have anticipated a situation like
this. In a way I had anticipated it – on all those evenings at
Mayburn Court when I sensed the tenuous nature of my happiness. But it was hard to accept that this was the end – of his
life, his creativity, and our friendship. My immediate concern,
however, was simply to get Emma and Surinder safely home,
and somehow I managed to do that. Leaving Emma with Jim,
I went along to Archie and Elizabeth's to ask if they knew
what had happened or if they had received any further news
from George's family. Then I went back to Ness and talked
to Jim, going over and over my last moments with George; he
listened patiently. After a few hours, Fraser Dixon rang to say
that George had passed away. My journal entry for that day is

brief: 'Katrina is 2. Hopedale at 10 a.m. GMB died 5.50 p.m.'
I have no memory of what I said or felt at the moment when
Fraser told me the news. Later, when I was upstairs with Emma,
Archie and his son Graham came to the house, thinking I might
not have heard that George had gone. Jim called out to me and
I went down to the kitchen where they were waiting, and I
put my arms around them both in an awkward, silent embrace:
there seemed to be nothing to say.

When I think of the weeks that followed, my lasting impression is one of a curious state of numbness. Even my lovely
daughter could hardly lift my spirits. There were some fine
spring days and evenings, but their beauty pained me. When
I first knew George, there were those moments sitting beside
his fire when I sensed what it might mean to lose him, but in
later years I had been taking him for granted. I think I realised,
long before he died, that in one sense I had already lost him –
lost the lovely, companionable friendship I once had with him
– through my own failure to show him how much he meant
to me; through my relationship with Jim; through Surinder's
arrival in Orkney; and simply because my life had changed –
and I had changed too.

When I stood in St Magnus Cathedral on the day of George's
funeral (which was also St Magnus Day), I had somehow never
felt so far removed from him, though this feeling is hard to
account for now. George was a famous writer who had many
friends and relations and admirers; consequently there were
hundreds of people there to pay homage, and a number of
them had known and loved George for many years. Some of
them were famous too. I remember seeing one man, a writer,
with tears running down his face, and my own grief seemed

an almost insignificant ripple in this massive flood of emotion. Kevin Crossley-Holland once remarked how much George was loved within his community; perhaps this was never more apparent than at his funeral.[29]

It was a historic occasion in more ways than one, marking the death of a national figure and also, as Ron Ferguson noted, 'only the second Requiem Mass in the nave of the cathedral since the Reformation'.[30] Presbyterian and Catholic clergy officiated, including Ron himself and Bishop Mario Conti, who sometimes visited Stromness; George mentioned him in a letter to Moira Burgess in July the previous year, telling her that 'Bishop Conti is coming to preach in St Magnus tomorrow. He'll come to Stromness to say Mass at 6 p.m.'[31] One of the few things that I recall clearly about the service, apart from the crowds of people crammed into the cathedral, is Max playing 'Farewell to Stromness' and breaking our hearts – I can't hear it without tears, even today.[32]

After the service I didn't want to go to George's interment at the Warebeth cemetery. Jim and I had left Emma with friends and I knew that she was perfectly safe, but in my emotional state I felt a pressing need to get back to her, and perhaps I simply could not face the thought of seeing dear George lowered into the ground. We had an early tea with Dorrie and Donald, and later that evening, before it got dark, I walked along the shore path to the cemetery and went through the lower gate to find George's burial place, next to his parents, which was covered with fresh earth and flowers. It was an evening of astonishing stillness and brilliance, and the setting sun blazed across Hoy Sound in a last surge of light, before night fell on a world that seemed strangely empty.

5

AFTER GEORGE

The past is not dead, it is living in us.[1]
William Morris

Over the years I have come to believe that death can never be a complete ending, however much it might feel like one. George's body was lying at peace in the earth, and his spirit was surely in heaven – or so I and many other people believed – but all those who loved him were left with their grief and their regrets, and a sense, in my own case at least, of unfinished business. The rapidity of his decline had left me feeling unprepared; I wasn't ready to say goodbye to him.

In the immediate aftermath of George's death, it seemed impossible to open a newspaper without finding an obituary or an article about him. That should have been comforting, but in truth I found it an ordeal because I did not want to accept that George had gone. I could hardly face reading these pieces; I would begin, but find them too painful. I was shaken by details of his life that were completely new to me. It was a revelation, for example, to find that George had been to Ireland in 1968

– he never mentioned it, even though we once talked about my visit in the 1980s to Dublin and to Thoor Ballylee, Yeats's home in County Galway; or there would be something that I thought inaccurate, such as a writer overemphasising George's dislike of the modern world by declaring that he had 'resisted installing a telephone', which might be taken to imply that he never had one.[2]

Then there were the photographs chosen to accompany the obituaries. In many of them George appears doleful, gloomy or even fierce. The worst, I thought, was the one chosen by *The Herald*,[3] in which he looked mournful, weary and bleary-eyed, resting his chin on his hand and giving the impression of being slightly the worse for drink. The same photograph was reproduced twelve days later in colour on the cover of *The Herald Weekend Extra*,[4] but inside, by way of compensation, was a much more pleasing picture of George in his rocking chair. The *Weekend Extra* also included several previously unpublished poems which were about to appear in the collection *Following a Lark*, including George's poem for Emma, 'A New Child: ECL'. *The Scotsman* used a wonderful photograph taken by Gunnie Moberg, showing George smiling and serene (a copy of it still hangs on the wall of my study), and two days later the same newspaper printed a striking picture by Orkney photographer Ken Amer, of pall-bearers lowering George's coffin into the grave.[5]

It is only now, reading the obituaries again all these years after George's death, that I can see them objectively and appreciate them fully. When I first looked at them, my sadness served as a distorting lens: I was over-sensitive, too critical, focusing on negative things and small errors. It was the tendency to place emphasis on George's dark days of depression that I found so perplexing. Although I had seen him at a very low ebb, that was not my lasting impression of him, and it was not the way that I would have wished him to be remembered. I had somehow overlooked one of the best pieces, written for *The Guardian*[6] by Joy Hendry (the editor of *Chapman*). She described a 'reticent, considerate, loving man'. An article in *The Independent* that caused me disproportionate distress at the time seems less wounding now. It claimed that 'despite his warm humour . . . one sensed an underlying sadness. Especially in the last few years of his life, Brown suffered from bouts of depression so acute that he sometimes longed for oblivion.'[7] Why, I ask myself, should this have made me feel so wretched and shocked when I first read it? Had George himself not told me – and written in his letters from Aberdeen – of his depression and his dark hours? Yet, thinking of the cheerful companion he had been to me, especially during the first year or so of our acquaintance, I found it hard to reconcile the smiling man in my memories with the melancholy figure portrayed in newsprint, who no longer cared to continue living.

I withdrew into myself for a while – in so far as that is possible when one has a small child. I don't know whether George's other friends were meeting, or talking to one another on the telephone, but I saw little of them, apart from Surinder. A line from Yeats's poem 'The Second Coming' used to run through my head: 'Things fall apart; the centre cannot hold'. An affection for George had brought disparate people together, and now that he was absent from the heart of the circle we were drifting apart; it is a matter of lasting regret to me that I lost touch with the Grants. I was comforted a little by a letter of condolence from my parents, written by my father, which ended: 'He has been such a good friend to you – in fact he was one of the first you made in Orkney. And he always made us feel welcome. We realise how much you will miss him – our deepest sympathy, my dear.'[8] I had always known I would miss George, but not how much. I have a vivid memory of kneeling on the floor with George's letters in my lap, wanting to read them again but afraid of the emotions they would stir, and putting them back unread into the drawer where they were kept.

At this difficult time, Maggie Parham – who had written the article in *The Independent* and who later, as Maggie Fergusson, was George's official biographer – arrived in Orkney. She came to Ness Road at the beginning of May, just two weeks after George's funeral, but I have no memory at all of how the visit came to be arranged. It was not a great success. For my part, it seemed too soon and too painful to be picking through my memories of George, especially with someone whom I had met only once before. We had been introduced when Maggie called at Pam Beasant's house with Matilda Tumim when I was there for coffee one morning, perhaps when she came to Orkney in 1995 to interview George.[9] If I had known then that Maggie was a friend of Renée's, I would probably have felt even more inhibited, but it wasn't until a year after George's death that I saw her reference to 'my 96-year-old friend Renée Simm' in the *Telegraph Weekend Magazine*.[10]

During our meeting I mentioned how important Nora had been to George (Maggie appeared to know little about Nora at that stage), but suggested that Nora might feel, as I did, that this was not the right time for an interview. I also told her – with unintended tactlessness – that some of the obituaries, and especially one, had distressed me because I hadn't been able to find in them the person I thought I knew. It was only after she left that I realised she had written the *Independent* piece. Maggie insisted that the darker picture was, overall, the more accurate one and explained to me that in George's autobiography, *For the Islands I Sing* (which she had already read, although it was not yet published), he had written of wishing for death ('one longs for oblivion').[11] It is hard to account for the anguish I felt on hearing this. Reading George's autobiography, and then his biography when it was published a decade later, I was able to accept that I hadn't understood how much he suffered, even to the point of longing for his life to end; I had never grasped or acknowledged the extent of his desperation, in spite of the letter he wrote to me from Aberdeen in September 1991, from which I have already quoted: 'I was quite exhausted in the end, and darkly depressed – much worse than any previous depression.' A conversation about rats came back to haunt me: I recalled the evening at Mayburn Court when George talked to me about how his house had been invaded by them: how he could hear them scrabbling behind the walls at night and he thought they were in the airing cupboard; how they kept him awake. I had tried to be practical and positive, suggesting that we should contact the council and reassuring him that the wretched creatures would soon be gone. But as I remembered his deep gloom, I thought that perhaps the rats, although certainly very real, were also connected with a sense of despair and foreboding, and I fretted that I hadn't picked up on this at the time.

I wasn't alone in my failure to recognise George's depression; Fergusson remarks upon how well he was able to hide his feelings from his friends, even those who were close to him and thought that they understood him, and she writes that 'neither Norrie's widow, Hazel Brown, nor George's brother Jackie knew anything of his depressive tendencies until after his death. Gerry Meyer, whose friendship with George dates back to the early days of the war, only once had an inkling of them.'[12]

Many of my recollections of the weeks after George's death are hazy, and I had all but abandoned the idea of keeping a diary. Nevertheless, there are notes here and there to remind me that life did go on. Surinder came to see me at Ness Road shortly after George's funeral – we talked about George, of course – and again a few days later to have tea with us. It was Jim's fortieth birthday at the end of April and we went out for a celebratory dinner at the Foveran, a restaurant just outside Kirkwall. But what I remember most clearly is that in the subsequent months, my daily walks to Emma's playgroup, the shops and the doctor's surgery all involved going past George's empty house. Even in the daytime and on light summer evenings this was unsettling, but as the autumn drew on and his windows remained dark at night it seemed to become even more difficult to walk by without feeling sad. I would look up at the closed door and the blank panes – across which no curtains were drawn, behind which no lamp shone – and picture the emptiness inside.

I went into the house only once after George's death, on a final visit that was suggested by Allison Dixon, who still had a key. She asked me if I would like a last look at the place where I had spent so many happy hours, and I met her at Mayburn Court on an October afternoon when the light was just beginning to fade; she unlocked the door and I followed her in. The first thing I saw was one of George's coats, still hanging – as it had always hung – on a row of pegs in the hall, together with a collection of woollen scarves knitted by his admirers. The sight smote my heart and I buried my face in the coat, seeking the comforting smell of George: of wool and tea and smoke from the hearth. An evocative photograph taken by Angela Catlin in 1985, for the book *Natural Light: Portraits of Scottish Writers*, shows George standing in front of those coat pegs, and I felt a surge of emotion when I first saw it in 2014. The picture is captioned 'The Seller of Old Coats' and George provided the accompanying text, which expresses a certain hopelessness about the future of poetry, but reveals his wry humour and his ability to make fun of himself:

> Where will there ever be a singer to enchant the ears of the people until they turn away from *Coronation Street*? Where is the Pied Piper of the late 20th century, who will take us from the spoliation of the earth's resources (and wild sweet beauties) and the stock-piles of atomic death, and show us again Hesperides, Tir-Nan-Og, the Land of the Young?
>
> Not this bard. What is the use of words, if they only add to the desert? So he opened instead a booth for the sale of second hand clothes. And along came a nice photographer called Angela from Glasgow and she took this picture of the old-clothes man waiting for a customer to show up.[13]

On that day when I visited Mayburn Court with Allison, there was almost nothing else left in the house. The sitting room seemed shockingly bare, stripped of most of the furniture and of George's belongings. In the kitchen, the larder door stood ajar; a pile of odd saucers sat on a shelf. Allison came upstairs with me and we stood in silence for a few minutes in George's bedroom, still furnished with his bed and a chest of drawers. I had been in that room only once before, when George asked me to help him move a heater, and I had been slightly taken aback by its spartan character. For his seventieth birthday I had given him a brightly coloured Indian wool rug so that he would have something warm to put his feet on when he got out of bed, but that was no longer there. Allison Dixon and I have never been close friends, but she had an instinctive grasp of what George meant to me and of how distraught I was at his death. She let me take away an old brown corduroy jacket and a mustard-coloured pullover which we found in the chest of drawers, just so that I would have something of his for comfort at that time of still-raw emotions – the pullover might have been the one George is wearing in the picture taken at Bessie Grieve's house. I eventually gave the pullover and the jacket to Stromness Museum for an exhibition, *Just George: George Mackay Brown, Poet & Author 1921–1996*, which opened in March 2006, and it was wonderful to see a few of George's other belongings there, including his rocking chair and the embroidered wall-hanging that I had so often admired. Janette Park, the curator of the Orkney Museum, told me in the spring of 2014 that the jacket and pullover had just been all the way to Shetland, as part of the *Writing the North* exhibition at the Shetland Museum and Archives, and I imagined George smiling to himself about this.

I did have something else tangible by which to remember George, as Phyllis Brown invited me to call at her house in Alfred Street, a while after his death, to collect something of his that she had put aside for me. She had chosen a small pot, about three inches high with a blue-and-white glaze; some words had been inscribed by George's own hand onto the clay: 'A peedie [then a word I'm unable to decipher] for mayflowers, seapinks, marigolds. GMB'. I remembered seeing a stack of similarly engraved pots and bowls and plates on the bookshelves behind the sofa at Mayburn Court, waiting for the potter Andrew Appleby to collect them and take them back to Fursbreck Pottery.

From time to time since our marriage, Jim and I had discussed the possibility of moving away from Orkney – we both had family on the mainland, and I always knew that he might not want to remain at the Academy for the rest of his career. Yet when the subject came up again that summer I was distressed. In one way it would have been a good time to go south, to make a different kind of life for ourselves, but unhappy people can become too self-absorbed and I had an underlying sense of being more closely bound to Orkney than ever before. My irrational belief was that if I went away, I would feel even further removed from George. I would certainly not have refused to go, but I was secretly relieved that nothing came up to tempt Jim away from Stromness.

George had been very much a part of Emma's life too, and she became convinced that he was living with us, as I recorded in a notebook: 'After George's death she is slightly disturbed – inevitably – & keeps saying that he is here, in the house . . . We talk a lot about heaven – but she says George isn't in heaven, he lives here now . . .'. One evening, she and I were in her room at bedtime and suddenly she looked up and said 'George is here.' I have often wondered what she might have seen or sensed, but she was so young then that she is unable to recall that moment.

I had no such visions of George, but he continued to be a part of my life, just as he still is a part of it. During that first summer without him, there were many fine evenings when I

THE SEED BENEATH THE SNOW

walked to his grave at Warebeth, and those visits were sources of pleasure as well as times of sadness and regret. Lapwings called out joyfully, and in a narrow burn full of water running off the fields I once saw a glint of blue – a lark's egg, snagged in the streaming grasses. On another occasion I fell into step with a woman whom I knew only slightly, and before long we found ourselves deep in an intense conversation about our daughters. Sometimes I went by the shore path, sometimes down the Netherton Road, always with the view of Hoy ahead of me, and Hoy Sound opening to the wider ocean beyond. As the weather became wilder, the landscape became bleaker; the bleached grasses lay in broken swathes, the fields were sodden and the ditches full of brown water. In the winter I didn't venture there for weeks on end, but on freezing nights I often thought of George, lying in his cold bed under the snow.

For some time, George's burial place was marked only by the gravestone for his parents ('John Brown / 1875–1940 / Taylor and Postman / Mary Brown / 1891–1967'), but before long the site began to acquire a collection of tributes: an oval red stone from Rackwick, pottery jars full of garden flowers, pebbles from the West Shore, and a handful of shells. When I visited the grave on his birthday in October I went empty-handed, but later added my own offering to this medley – a small earthenware pot that had once held honey, filled with crocuses from our garden, to mark the coming of the first spring since George's death. It was an unpleasant shock when all these treasures vanished – removed, perhaps, by someone who felt the need to tidy up (the cemetery is well kept, the grass cut regularly) or who thought that these rather higgledy-piggledy declarations of love and admiration were not in keeping with

George's status as a famous poet. Eventually a beautiful, simple slab appeared, bearing his name, the word 'POET', his dates, four symbols and some words from one of his poems ('CARVE THE RUNES / THEN BE CONTENT WITH SILENCE'), cut by the artist Frances Pelly.[14]

I am clearly not alone in having found consolation in visiting George's grave. I knew perfectly well that it was merely the husk of George – to borrow from his own imagery – that was lying in the earth at Warebeth cemetery, but it felt important to visit the place where he was still physically present, even if to do so reinforced the knowledge that the friend I had loved was no longer in the world. In the muddle of grief, it took me a while to understand that George's story was far from over. No more marvellous words would flow from his pen, but the corpus of his published work remained, solid and magnificent, to delight and inspire generations of readers, and he also left a store of unpublished writings, some of which are now in print – and one hopes that more of these will appear in the future.

George is still very much a presence in Stromness. A lovely memorial garden has been made at the south end of the town, near the Double Houses; his rocking chair is displayed in the museum; a fellowship was set up in his name in 2006 to promote creative writing in Orkney and to celebrate Orkney writers, past and present.[15] I often see tourists pausing at Mayburn Court to photograph the blue plaque that commemorates his residence there; it is set high up on the wall, out of harm's way. I think it might amuse George to know that another plaque, at his birthplace on Clouston's Pier, was stolen – presumably by an over-ardent fan – although I knew nothing of this until Brian Murray recently told me the story.

In the past two decades there have been many events connected with George, to serve as memorials to his life and work. In June 1996, two months after his death, the Pier Arts Centre held an exhibition of Gunnie Moberg's work and hosted the launch of the collaborative work by Gunnie and George, *Orkney: Pictures and Poems*.[16] The following January, Yvonne Gray (Orkney Arts Society's next literature secretary) organised the annual winter Foy, and this time it was centred around George. According to the programme, all the writers taking part had 'received encouragement and advice from the poet or . . . been influenced by his work: the evening is, therefore, a tribute to his generosity and his inspiration'. Yvonne asked me if I would read, with John Aberdein, Pam Beasant and Magnus Dixon (George's great-nephew), and music was provided by the oboist Christina Sargent.

I began with George's poem 'A New Child' and then read four poems dedicated to him: 'Evening Visit', 'The Guest', 'After George' and 'Images'. I had written the first of these when George was still alive, but never shown it to him, and the other three came to me in the months after his death. I agonised over submitting them to *Chapman* for publication, wondering if George would approve of making these essentially private emotions more widely known, and I was just as hesitant about reading them to an audience. As I began, I was aware that my hands were shaking, and matters were not helped by the fact that Renée Simm was sitting in the front row, leaning forward with her hand up to her ear to catch my words as I stumbled through the lines, including one about holding George's hand in a taxi.

I was feeling more kindly towards Renée then, understanding

that George's passing would have left a great void in her life. I even visited her at Quildon Cottage, as I mentioned earlier, and although I have no recollection at all of how I came to be there, I know that I would not have gone without being asked. It is an interesting house, an early nineteenth-century listed building with a former grain-drying kiln at one end of it, and I went on a sunny Saturday morning when the back door was wide open so that light streamed in. As I recall – although not clearly – there were lovely pieces of pottery (perhaps made by Bernard Leach) on high shelves, and pictures on the walls. In the space which had once been the kiln stood a striking life-size sculpture of a boy, by William Lamb. Renée's vivid green tracksuit was certainly unforgettable, and her thinning white hair, that I had only ever seen twisted into a knot, was hanging loose. Her feet were bare and I noticed that they were smooth and shapely, like those of a much younger woman – she would have been in her late nineties then.

Renée made coffee, and the conversation ran smoothly for a while until she began to berate me about a friend of mine who had moved far away from where her parents lived. Renée's view was that this was very selfish behaviour, and I became slightly heated in defending my friend, well aware that I had done exactly the same thing. A full-blown argument was narrowly avoided, and I wasn't invited to Quildon Cottage again. Renée moved away from Orkney for her last years and died in 2005 at the age of 104.

Not long after the Foy for George, I was coming up the steps from our pier one afternoon, on my way to meet Emma from nursery school, when a car drew up and the driver asked if I knew where Gunnie Moberg lived. I gave directions to the Don and mentioned that our house had once been Gunnie and Tam's home. The driver and his passenger seemed interested to hear this and introduced themselves as Julian May from BBC Radio 4 and the poet Kevin Crossley-Holland, and they explained that they were in Orkney to interview people about George for a documentary, 'Interrogating Silence', part of the *Kaleidoscope* series. When they heard that I too had known George, they asked whether they might come back the next day and talk to me. They duly arrived at Ness Road and we drank tea and spent some time reminiscing about George, whom Kevin had known for many years. I also showed them the handwritten copy of 'A New Child' and Kevin asked if I would read it aloud for the tape recorder.

Amongst the other voices in the programme were those of Kevin himself; the writer and essayist Ronald Blythe; the playwright Alan Plater; Maggie Parham; Archie Bevan and Ron Ferguson. We also heard from Gunnie Moberg, who spoke about travelling to London with George, and about his responses to her photographs when they worked together on *Orkney: Pictures and Poems*; and Jack Rendall from Rackwick, for whose daughter the lovely 'Lullaby for Lucy' was written by George and Max ('Rowan and lamb and waters salt and sweet / Entreat the / New child to the brimming / Dance of the valley'). Then there was fisherman Willie Sinclair, saying that what he missed most about George was 'his piece in the *Orcadian* every week, all about Stromness', followed by my brief reminiscences and my reading of 'A New Child'; and, most movingly for me, Max, speaking from Hopedale, I think, over the poignant notes of 'Farewell to Stromness':

Knowing that George was there, working away in Stromness here, there was a kind of continuity; you knew somebody else was battling away with the elements, with a language, creating something wonderful. When I come into Stromness on the boat – I know I always used to look for George's house and think, well, George is in there, I wonder what he's working on, what joy is going to come out later this year, when you see the result of his present labour. And now you come in on the *St Ola* and you look – and it's *not* the same. There's a gap.

Hearing these words brought back something else: I remembered that at George's funeral, Father Spencer had described in a similar way what George's presence in Orkney had meant to him: when he was on the boat, coming into Stromness harbour, he would think: 'George is here, George is here!'

The programme ended with Kevin climbing the steps at Mayburn Court and commenting that George's window 'is dark on the inside . . . But he was *loved* in his community; his work is read, on the islands and off the islands, in many different countries. So – all right, the window may be dark, but in the meantime old George has lit a light and I don't think it's going to go out.'

'Interrogating Silence' was broadcast on a Saturday evening, 21 February 1998. My father, hundreds of miles away in Kent, listened to it and we spoke on the telephone the following day. He was never particularly at ease on the phone and so our conversations tended to be brief, in spite of the affection between us, but on this occasion he talked to me at length, wanting to tell me how much he had enjoyed the programme.

'I couldn't have done it better myself', he teased. He died quite unexpectedly of a heart attack on the following Thursday, at the age of eighty-two. I discovered afterwards that on 25 February, the day before his death, he wrote to my sister Judy in Australia, telling her that I had been on the radio 'for about four minutes . . . reminisced about George and read the poem he'd written when Emma was born. A great thrill and a proud one.'

The years passed and yet somehow George was always present, in all kinds of ways. One day I received a package containing an exquisite book, *Sister Margaret Tournour*, by David Burnett.[17] It was a gift from an acquaintance living in Penzance, whom I had met only briefly when she visited my house with mutual friends. She wrote that when she came across the book she immediately thought of her visit to Stromness and my connection with George; it is an account of the life of a remarkable nun and artist who had a poem, 'St Magnus Day 1992',[18] dedicated to her by George, with whom she had corresponded.

In the autumn of 2007 I went to Sutherland for a long weekend and stayed in a small guest house just outside Tongue. On the last morning, my companion was glancing at a copy of *The Northern Times* and saw an article by Raymond Train, 'George Mackay Brown – Norseman and Gael'.[19] The main photograph illustrating the article was captioned 'The ruins of George Mackay Brown's mother's home at Brawl, near Strathy'.[20] Brawl was not many miles along the road, only a slight detour from our route back to the ferry; it was too good an opportunity to miss and we had plenty of time, so we turned off the main road and drove until we reached the place shown in the photograph. It was easy to recognise the spot and we were able to park close to the roofless, crumbling walls of what had once been Mhairi Mackay's home. I was profoundly moved, not only because this was a place with which George had such a direct connection, and which he had visited, but because the dimensions of the house clearly revealed the comparative poverty and cramped conditions in which his mother must have grown up.

Several months after this, Archie Bevan (in his capacity as George's literary executor) received a letter from Beth Griffiths in Surrey, who had been trying to track down a poem that she remembered having heard on the radio a decade earlier. 'Some years ago', she wrote, 'I heard a radio programme about George Mackay Brown. I was very struck by one particular poem written for a neighbour upon the birth of her daughter. It welcomed the new baby and made an analogy of laying down the ribs for a new boat and the growth of the new child.' She was referring to 'Interrogating Silence' and to my reading of 'A New Child'. Beth had searched for the poem once before, without success, but after the birth of her own first grandchild, Josie, she was determined to find it. She borrowed George's *Collected Poems* from the library, but it is a large volume and she was unable to discover the lines she half remembered. 'It is many years since I heard it', she added in her letter, 'so it may be entirely different to my memory.' Elizabeth Bevan replied promptly, and Beth went back to the library and took out *Collected Poems* once more:

I turned to page 328 as I walked home and the hairs went up on the back of my neck. The poem is far more beautiful than I remember. The splinters that are rain, the seapinks and daisies are wonderful and unremembered. But the great theme: the voyage and the keel, strakes, mast, sail and chart had somehow remained. They are the theme and framework of the poem and the future life of the child. It still makes me shiver ... Could that original radio documentary have gone out 10 years ago or more? If so, it says a great [deal] for Mackay Brown's imagery that a single hearing can persist for such a long time.[21]

I felt inordinately happy to know that George's lovely poem for Emma had made such an impact. Elizabeth let me borrow Beth's letter so that I could photocopy it, and when I saw Beth's telephone number at the top I rang her on an impulse. She told me how phrases from the poem had stayed with her for more than a decade; we talked about her family and I promised to send her a tape-recording of the radio programme so that she could listen to it again. When I was writing a first draft of this chapter, I contacted Beth to ask for permission to quote from her letter, which she gave willingly: 'Of course you can quote my letter ... please don't change the "hairs went up on my neck" bit, because that really happened.'[22]

Some years later, looking at the George Mackay Brown website set up by Sue Vickers Tordoff, I was delighted to find three lines from what I think of as 'Emma's poem' at the top of the 'Timeline' page: 'The boat / Will take a few summers to build / That you must make your voyage in'.[23]

In the autumn of 2009, Ron Ferguson telephoned to ask if he might interview me as part of his research for the book he was writing about George.[24] Sitting with Ron in my study, talking about George and revisiting the events of two decades earlier, I joked about how the room was a sort of shrine to GMB, full of relics. As I pointed out pictures and objects to Ron, I was strongly aware, yet again, of how much George was still part of my life. The wonderful, smiling photograph of him taken by Gunnie Moberg that had accompanied his obituary in *The Scotsman* was displayed on the wall above my desk; the picture of him sitting beside me at Bessie Grieve's house hung above one end of the mantelpiece, and at the other end was a framed copy of the poem 'Lux Perpetua', printed on fine paper and sent to us by George as a Christmas card.[25] A drawer was full of letters and acrostics from him, and newspaper cuttings about him. His presence had spread into other rooms, too: his books filled a shelf in the living room upstairs, and *A Stone Calendar* displayed the months.[26] The precious framed manuscript of his poem for Emma was hanging on her bedroom wall. All these things still remain in the house at Ness Road. Wherever I may live in the future, they will be part of my surroundings – except for the original manuscript of 'A New Child', which I'm sure Emma will want to take to her own home one day.

Chance meetings and conversations can still bring George to the forefront of my mind. Visiting an exhibition at the Pier Arts Centre early in 2010, I overheard a woman (perhaps Sigrid Appleby) in the next room say to her companion: 'I wonder what George would have made of this?' At another exhibition, at Tankerness House Museum in Kirkwall, I saw Jocelyn Rendall from Papa Westray. She mentioned Ron Ferguson's forthcoming book on George, explaining that she had been transcribing the taped interviews that Ron conducted as part of his research, and we talked about some poems that George had written for *The Tablet*. More recently, in the spring of 2014, I went to Brian and Liza Murray's house at Hoymansquoy and we sat drinking tea and discussing old times, and George seemed to be there among us again – I could almost hear his voice. In June, at a St Magnus Festival poetry event, I sat next to a visitor who suddenly began to speak about George, telling me about the time when she and her husband had been sitting next to him on a bench near the bookshop and conversed with him, without knowing who he was; they discovered his identity afterwards, when they went into the shop and Tam enlightened them. And just days later, as I walked past the bookshop, a man stopped in his tracks, pointed to a book displayed in the window (it was *Rockpools and Daffodils*, with a picture of George on the cover) and said to his young son, 'That's George Mackay Brown', in a tone of great respect – almost reverence – that touched me deeply.

Thus, everywhere I turn, there is still something to remind me of George, and I see how his life has left its marks – on me and on the place where I live. I often wonder what he would have thought of all the changes in Stromness, and in my own life. Towards the end, he said to me that when he went along the street he was struck by how many new faces there were, how many people he didn't know, especially the children, and this is echoed in 'Under Brinkie's Brae': 'As one gets older, one lives in a town of strangers, increasingly.'[27] He would surely have been happy to see Emma growing into a young woman with a love of literature and history and art, and to know that she would study English literature at the University of Edinburgh (in her second year she lived in a flat in Marchmont Crescent, a few doors away from where George once lived during his time in Edinburgh). I would have found it difficult, however, to tell him in 2001 that Jim and I had decided to live apart, after ten years of marriage, although we are friends to this day and I am sure we always will be, with Emma as our shared focus. I like to think that George would have been kind and non-judgemental, but this would have been a hard thing to say to him; I can imagine that shuttered, slightly cold expression passing across his face, even if only for a moment.

There have been other changes too: the black dog tormented me cruelly for a while, but I was given the help I needed and I hope that I have seen it off for good. I spent a decade cleaning houses and working as a gardener to earn a living. Now I copy-edit books and journal articles, working from home in the room filled with pictures and memorabilia of George, his face smiling down at me when I glance up from the computer screen.

In writing this history of my friendship with George, I have given what is necessarily a partial account because it is primarily a personal one, based largely on my own recollections, though I am grateful to Moira Burgess, Carl MacDougall, Brian and Liza Murray and others who have shared their anecdotes, photographs and letters with me. My memories are anchored by letters written to me by George, my diaries and notebooks of the period, my letters to my parents, and a collection of newspaper cuttings and Foy programmes. Why write the book at all, some might ask, when a perfectly good biography of George's whole life has already been published, not to mention other extensive works on his writing and his faith? I had often considered the possibility of gathering together my stories and thoughts about George, but it was a comment made by Moira Burgess in a Christmas card sent to me in 2006, about the official biography and its coverage of the last years of George's life, that finally motivated me to do something. It seemed that writing things down might serve several purposes, one of which – as I outlined in the introduction – would be to provide a background for 'A New Child' and an explanation for Emma of why a man whom she hardly remembers wrote this affectionate poem for her. Another would be to contribute something to the store of tales about George, to add a few more brushstrokes to the portrait of this complex man; and yet another might be to fill in several gaps in the chronology of his last decade – by describing, for example, some of the local readings, private views and social occasions that he attended. Even if his later years were less eventful (and this may be true of many lives), it does not necessarily follow that they were without importance. When we are young, it can seem as if all the significant things that are going to happen to us will happen before we grow old or even middle-aged. The published accounts of George's earlier life are rich in event and detail – his childhood in Stromness, his time in Edinburgh, his relationship with Stella Cartwright – and it would be easy to overlook the interests and the more subdued emotions of his final decade. George himself set the precedent for this, by writing in the appendix to his autobiography that nothing of much significance happened to him after 1985.

When I began to explore the idea of a book about George, one acquaintance – who had grown up in Stromness and known George since she was a child – said, perhaps rather dismissively, that everyone in Stromness had their own stories about him. That may be true, but I wondered how many people would be willing to share their tales and write them down for posterity. It is so easy to put off the task. In Aberdeen Royal Infirmary in 2002, having major surgery after the discovery of a second and more sinister ovarian tumour, I realised how quickly we can be overtaken by events. We may have less time than we think. Nora and Gunnie both passed away in 2007 (Nora in August and Gunnie in October).[28]

I deferred reading Maggie Fergusson's definitive biography of George for quite a long while. Everyone else I knew in Stromness seemed to have read it, and the general consensus was very favourable. Yet I feared that no matter how interesting and elucidating it might turn out to be, to encounter George again within its pages and to discover things he might have preferred to keep private would be an uncomfortable experience. And so it was, in some ways. Over the years I had met some of the people mentioned in the biography, and I was familiar with many of the events it describes, having heard about them from George himself or from his friends and relations, but there was also a great deal that I had never known or even suspected about this essentially reserved person who had once been my friend. It was as if, in reading the biography, I was confronted with a man quite unlike the one I met in 1988, and this experience was both illuminating and disconcerting.

Fergusson explores the last decade of George's life less thoroughly than she does the earlier years, and this is understandable to a certain extent: as I have suggested, it is often the case that fewer of the more important events of our lives will take place during our later years. Yet out of almost three hundred pages of text (in the paperback edition, and excluding the notes and index), only fifteen of them cover the last seven years. Fergusson begins that final chapter by wondering 'what further adventures George might have enjoyed, had his health not begun to fail him' in 1989.[29] As I hope this book has illustrated, George's last decade was not uneventful; nor was it unproductive, and

THE SEED BENEATH THE SNOW

Archie Bevan and Brian Murray are surely right to claim, in their introduction to *Travellers*, that 'his delight in writing was undiminished'.[30]

It was rather a shock, when reading Fergusson's biography, to discover that I had vanished completely from George's life. My name was not mentioned anywhere, not even in passing, and I found it oddly painful to be thus excluded. So perhaps an underlying motivation for writing this book was not only to give the backstory of Emma's poem and to keep my recollections of George safe and fixed in print, but also to attempt to free myself from a sense of having been written out of his history. It has taken me far too long to put together these chapters; my progress has been interrupted by the challenges of parenthood and the need to find work and earn a living, and for a while I was preoccupied by my mother's increasing frailness and her death. When I began, I did not know that Ron Ferguson was planning a book about George, but in reading his detailed exploration of George's life and faith I was glad to find myself placed firmly within the circle again and named in the 'roll-call of servants' who tended to George's needs: 'Joanna Ramsey was his driver and friend.'[31] That seems to sum it up rather well.

During the years since George's death, my visits to his grave gradually became less frequent as my sense of his presence slowly diminished. In the final weeks of working on this book, however, I have been going along the West Shore to the cemetery almost every day, early in the morning; it seems fitting to be making this pilgrimage to George. The wild flowers along the shore path are in their glory – red campion everywhere; purple and yellow vetches; birdsfoot trefoil half hidden in the grasses; buttercups and clover. George's favourites, the beautiful sea pinks, are fading now, as June turns to July. Great skuas pass overhead, and one morning two ravens watched from a promontory. The oystercatchers call noisily, drowning out the rippling lower note of the curlews across the fields, and at the cemetery they stand sentinel on several of the memorials, piping in alarm as I open the metal gate at the far end.

It is a strangely beautiful place, as George described: 'The legends of the dead, their carved names / Faced east, into the first light, among sea sounds'.[32] As I tread the grassy paths I notice the memorial to my kind neighbour Nora Wishart, and Granny and my dear friends Dorrie and Donald Morrison are lying at rest nearby. Reaching George's stone, I see that a little heap of beach pebbles and shells and sea glass is accumulating again beside it, and a miniature koala suggests a far longer pilgrimage than mine. There is a small penal cross, too, and a pen, and someone has left a posy of wild flowers. 'Is it all right with you, George?' I ask him, pausing for a few moments beside his grave, wondering what he would think about the publication of this book. I make my own answer out of the silence that is not silence at all, filled as it is with the pulse of the waves, the cries of birds, the faint singing of seals in Hoy Sound, the ceaseless flickering wind.

One memorable morning I set out feeling sure that the manuscript was finally complete, and found a rainbow arching from the Kame of Hoy to just beyond the cemetery wall – not pale and shifting, as Orkney rainbows often are, but vivid and persistent against the slate-grey sky. Make of it what you will, but to echo Ron Ferguson's words at George's funeral, referring to the fact that George was to be buried on St Magnus Day, 'If you call that a coincidence, I wish you a very dull life.'

George's name still comes up many times in conversations in Orkney and elsewhere. People quite often ask whether I knew him, and the most accurate reply may be 'Hardly at all', for the conclusion of this account of our relationship seems to be that he was a complex and essentially private person. Two lines of the poem that he wrote for me come to mind: 'Not that, in this time of "vanitas" / Anyone can *really* know another'. Perhaps I did not always understand him very well. But what I do know for certain is that he was a wonderful writer, a kind man, a good companion and an affectionate friend, and I am fortunate to have been part of his life for a while. I hope he would approve of the glimpse I have given of him here.

Appendix One

'TO JOANNA'

To Joanna

How comes this, Joanna? Slowly
Through a late summer, an autumn,
   A half winter, we have
   Come to know each other

(Not that, in this time of "Vanities"
Anyone can _really_ know another.
   But sometimes, among the shadows and rocks
   One rock utters brightness.

Someone has brought a jar, a fragrance lingers),
So now, when you leave the islands
   For London, a five-day absence, I think
   'This will be a drab weekend'.

                              GMB
                              31/1/89 — 1/2/89

      But don't _you_ have a drab weekend,
              Joanna —
              Love, George   X

Original handwritten manuscript of 'To Joanna'

Appendix Two

'A NEW CHILD'

EMMA CATHERINE LAWSON

I   Wait awhile, small voyager
       On the shore, with seapinks and
                       shells

       The boat
         Will take a few summers to build
      That you must make your
                    voyage in

II   You will learn the names.
      That golden light is "sun", "moon"
        The silver light
      That grows and dwindles.

      And the beautiful small splinters
        That wet the stones, "rain"

III   There is a voyage to make,
       A chant to read,
      But not yet, not yet.
        "Daisies" spill from your
                   fingers.
        The night daisies are "stars"

      There are "cats" on the pier.
        There are "gulls", "fish"

IV   The keel is laid, the strakes
        Will be set, in time.
      A tree is growing
        That will be a tall mast

      All about you, meantime
      The music of humanity,
        The dance of creation:
      All scored on the chant of the
                  voyage

V Listen long to stories and songs
   Of other islands, ports, people
   Till your ship is ready

   The voyage of EMMA to Tir-Nan-Og

   You will not miss that landfall

VI May Saint Magnus be on the shore
                             with you
    At the time of crabs and sillocks,
    At the time of mid-sea waves,
       The horizon music,
    And at the helm, a shining friend,
                          with you

VII And may The Star of The Sea
           shine on your voyage.

                    George Mackay Brown
                    11 June 1993

*Handwritten manuscript of 'Emma Catherine Lawson'. A later
version was published as 'A New Child: ECL'*

NOTES

INTRODUCTION

1. George Mackay Brown, 'To Joanna', signed 'GMB, 31/1/89 – 1/2/89', previously unpublished.
2. John Murray, 1996, pp. 16–17.

I   AN INCOMER

1. *For the Islands I Sing: An Autobiography* (Edinburgh: Polygon, 2008), pp. 169–174. All page numbers refer to this paperback edition.
2. 'A Writer's Day', from 'Poems for Kenna', in *The Collected Poems of George Mackay Brown* (London: John Murray, 2005), p. 241.
3. Jackie McGlone, 'Interview: Kenna Crawford, Artist', *Scotland on Sunday*, 29 April 2012.
4. Brown, *For the Islands I Sing*, pp. 170, 169.
5. Ibid., p. 170.
6. From 'One Star in the West', in Brown, *Following a Lark*, p. 85.
7. In George Mackay Brown, *Travellers: Poems* (London: John Murray, 2001), pp. 139–40.
8. Maggie Fergusson, *George Mackay Brown: The Life* (London: John Murray, 2007), p. 260. All page numbers refer to this paperback edition.
9. George Mackay Brown, *An Orkney Tapestry* (London: Victor Gollancz, 1969), p. 24.
10. Ibid., p. 25.

11. George Mackay Brown, *Northern Lights: A Poet's Sources* (Edinburgh: Polygon, 1999), p. 313. For a full account of George's trip to Shetland, see 'Shetland: A Search for Symbols', pp. 237–303; and 'Shetland Diary', pp. 305–329.

12. See Brown, *Collected Poems*: 'Elegy', p. 32; 'The Death of Peter Esson', p. 18; 'The Poet', p. 45.

13. *Sea Haven: Stromness in the Orkney Islands* (Orkney: Orkney Press for Stromness Community Council, 1992).

14. 'Billie Ramsey's Behaviour' and 'Consolation in Loneliness', in George Mackay Brown, *Letters to Gypsy* (Nairn: Balnain Books, 1990), pp. 62–63, 131.

15. 'Under Brinkie's Brae', *Orcadian*, 15 November 1973; see also 'The Giving of Names', in George Mackay Brown, *Letters from Hamnavoe* (London and Edinburgh: Steve Savage, 2002), p. 136. Back copies of *The Orcadian* are available on microfilm at the Orkney Library & Archive in Kirkwall.

16. 'Evening Visit', *Chapman*, no. 89–90 (1998), also in Joanna Ramsey, *In Memory of George Mackay Brown* (Glasgow: Galdragon Press, 1998) and *Orkney Arts Review*.

17. 'Under Brinkie's Brae', *Orcadian*, 5 March 1992; see also 'Swung Gently through the Years', in George Mackay Brown, *The First Wash of Spring* (London and Edinburgh: Steve Savage, 2006), p. 24.

18. 'Under Brinkie's Brae', *Orcadian*, 17 January 1980; see also 'A Treaty with the Earth', in George Mackay Brown, *Rockpools and Daffodils: An Orcadian Diary 1979–1991* (Edinburgh: Gordon Wright, 1992), p. 21. My thanks to Brian Murray for finding this mention of the wall-hanging.

19. 'Dead Men Walk', in Peter Haining (ed.), *The Clans of Darkness: Scottish Stories of Fantasy and Horror* (London: Gollancz, 1971); Moira Burgess, letter to JR, 9 June 2007.

20. 'Voice of Orkney', *Scots Magazine*, 104, no. 6, new series (March 1976), p. 614.

21. See 'Poets', in Brown, *Orkney Tapestry*, pp. 163–171.

22. *Orcadian*, 4 November 1993; see also 'Clouston's Pier', in Brown, *First Wash of Spring*, pp. 118–119.

23. Oil on board, c. 1960s. See *Sylvia Wishart: A Study* (Stromness: Pier Arts Centre, 2012), p. 24.

24. Erlend Brown to JR, 16 May 2014.

25. *Sylvia Wishart*, p. 18.

26. Cf. Fergusson, *Life*, p. 277.

27. Ibid., p. 105.

28. From 'Small Songs for the Beginning of Lent', in Brown, *Travellers*, p. 98.
29. 'Nora Kennedy', *Herald*, 23 August 2007.
30. 'A Rack of Flowers', in Fergusson, *Life*, pp. 237–257.
31. Elborn, 'Nora Kennedy'.
32. Ibid.
33. *For The Islands I Sing*, p. 145.
34. From George Mackay Brown, 'The Realms of Gold', in *Chapman*, special issue on GMB, no. 60 (Spring 1990), pp. 24–31.
35. In *A Time to Keep and Other Stories* (London: Hogarth Press, 1976), pp. 155–182.
36. Muir quoted in Bold, *George Mackay Brown*, Modern Writers series (Edinburgh: Oliver & Boyd, 1978), p. 64.
37. Penguin Books, 1986.
38. *Loaves and Fishes: Poems by George Mackay Brown* (London: Hogarth Press, 1959).
39. John Murray, 1988.
40. Bold, *George Mackay Brown*, p. 113.
41. Ibid., p. 73.
42. From 'Hamnavoe', in Brown, *Loaves and Fishes*, p. 23.
43. From 'December Day, Hoy Sound', in Brown, *Loaves and Fishes*, p. 14; and 'Helmsman', in George Mackay Brown, *Fishermen with Ploughs* (London: Hogarth Press, 1971), p. 21.
44. Ron Ferguson, *George Mackay Brown: The Wound and the Gift* (Edinburgh: St Andrew's Press, 2011).
45. Fergusson, *Life*, p. 280.
46. Ferguson, *Wound and the Gift*, p. xxviii.
47. *Orcadian*, 21 February 1991.
48. 'From Your Stromness Correspondent', *Hoy Sound*, 1997, pp. 7, 15.
49. 'Under Brinkie's Brae', *Orcadian*, 21 February 1991.
50. Presented by Kevin Crossley-Holland, produced by Julian May, BBC Radio 4, 21 February 1998.
51. 'Under Brinkie's Brae', *Orcadian*, 30 August 1990; see also 'A Wilderness of Paper', in Brown, *Rockpools and Daffodils*, p. 242.
52. 'Under Brinkie's Brae', *Orcadian*, 20 July 1995; see also 'Problem of Space and Shelf-room', in Brown, *First Wash of Spring*, p. 211.
53. A Norse word for a place where boats are hauled up in rough weather.
54. Brown, *For the Islands I Sing*, p. 73.
55. Ibid.
56. *Bookmaking: A Case Study of Publishing* (Scottish Film Council, 1988).

57. *Orcadian*, 8 September 1988.
58. From 'Does This Make Sense?' (1963), in Naomi Mitchison, *Essays and Journalism: Volume 2: Carradale*, edited by Moira Burgess (Glasgow: Kennedy & Boyd, 2009), p. 102.
59. Chatto & Windus/Hogarth Press, 1984.
60. Young Films, 1989, directed by Ian Sellar.
61. *Orcadian*, 21 July 1988.
62. *Orcadian*, 27 October 1988.
63. Ibid.
64. *Shoal and Sheaf: Orkney's Pictorial Heritage* (Kirkwall: Orkney Library, 1988).
65. Brown, *Orkney Tapestry*, p. 40.
66. Fergusson, *Life*, p. 203.
67. *Sidney Nolan, Paintings 1942–77*, Pier Arts Centre, Stromness, 10 June to 9 July 1989.
68. Moira Burgess to JR, notes on GMB, May 2014.
69. My thanks to Fiona Shaw for this information, and to Kathleen Luckey, Television Curator at the British Film Institute National Archive, for her help.
70. Ferguson, *Wound and the Gift*, pp. 353–354.
71. Fergusson, *Life*, p. 284, footnote.
72. Ferguson, *Wound and the Gift*, p. 349.
73. 'A Christmas Foy', *Orcadian*, 15 December 1988.
74. 'That's My Weakness Now', *Glasgow Herald*, 4 April 1988.
75. *Orcadian*, 17 November 1994; see also 'Salute the Hen', in Brown, *First Wash of Spring*, p. 176.
76. See Fergusson, *Life*, pp. 284–285. The poem appears in *Following a Lark*, p. 34.

2 A WIDENING CIRCLE

1. 5 January 1989.
2. See her obituary by Robert Cormack, *Herald*, 3 July 1997.
3. GMB to Moira Burgess, letter, 6 January 1989.
4. See Wikipedia entry for *Ivan's Childhood*, http://en.wikipedia.org/wiki/Talk%3AIvan's_Childhood.
5. An Orkney word for rubbish.
6. *Orcadian*, 5 July 1990; see also 'Festival Poets', in Brown, *Rockpools and Daffodils*, p. 239.
7. Gerry Cambridge to JR, note, 7 August 2000.

8. Brown, 'To Joanna'.
9. Fergusson, *Life*, p. 261.
10. 'Body Ashore: For a Child Who Drowned', *New Shetlander*, 189 (March 1992), p. 31.
11. Galloping Dog Press, 1991. For review, see *Orcadian*, 2 March 1989.
12. Moira Burgess to JR, notes on GMB, May 2014.
13. Moira Burgess, letter to *Scotsman*, 18 April 1996.
14. GMB to Moira Burgess, letter, 12 October 1989.
15. Moira Burgess to JR, notes on GMB, May 2014.
16. *Orcadian*, 9 March 1989; see also 'A Drive to Birsay', in Brown, *Rockpools and Daffodils*, pp. 206–207.
17. *Mishima: A Life in Four Chapters* (1985), directed by Paul Schrader.
18. *Orcadian*, 6 April 1989.
19. In *Chapman*, no. 89–90 (1998), and Ramsey, *In Memory of George Mackay Brown*.
20. *Orcadian*, 13 April 1989; see also 'Academy Library – Old and New', in Brown, *Rockpools and Daffodils*, p. 210.
21. Brown, *For the Islands I Sing*, p. 171.
22. Frank Richardson to JR, letter, 24 May 1989.
23. *Orcadian*, 27 April 1989. The event was funded by the Book Trust, Orkney Arts Society and British Airways.
24. 'Under Brinkie's Brae', *Orcadian*, 1 June 1989.
25. GMB to JR, postcard, 3 June 1989.
26. 'The View From Here: George Mackay Brown: Orkney', *Telegraph Weekend Magazine*, June 1989.
27. *Orcadian*, 29 June 1989.
28. Aberdeen University Press, 1985.
29. 'Orkney's Prospero', *Slightly Foxed* (Winter 2004), p. 39.
30. See 'Under Brinkie's Brae', *Orcadian*, 6 July 1989.
31. *Orcadian*, 16 March 1989.
32. 'Under Brinkie's Brae', *Orcadian*, 13 July 1989; see also 'Ecclesiastes', in Brown, *Rockpools and Daffodils*, p. 214.
33. See Fergusson, *Life*, pp. 154, 174, 175.
34. Ibid., p. 172.
35. *Sylvia Wishart: A Study*: see p. 108.
36. GMB to JR, letter from Aberdeen, 1 August 1989.
37. GMB to JR, letter from Aberdeen, 6 August 1989.
38. GMB to JR, letter from Aberdeen, 18 August 1989.
39. *Orcadian*, 31 May 1990; see also 'Home Thoughts from Hospital', in Brown, *Rockpools and Daffodils*, p. 237.

40. 'Under Brinkie's Brae', *Orcadian*, 17 August 1989.

41. *Orcadian*, 21 September 1989.

42. GMB to JR, letter from Aberdeen, 26 October 1989.

43. Carl MacDougall to JR, email, 14 May 2014.

44. *Orcadian*, 16 November 1989.

45. Mariscat Press, 1986.

46. Secker & Warburg, 1989.

47. Carl MacDougall to JR, email, 14 May 2014.

48. *Orcadian*, 30 November 1989.

49. Geoffrey Elborn, 'Nora Kennedy', *Herald*, 23 August 2007.

50. *Orcadian*, 23 November 1989; see also 'Return of the Rats', in Brown, *Rockpools and Daffodils*, p. 226.

51. 'A Christmas Foy: Orkney Poets at the Pier Arts Centre', *Orcadian*, 21 December 1989.

3   AMONG THE SHADOWS

1. Catherine Gordon, one of Elaine and Alistair Gordon's daughters.

2. Keith Allardyce to JR, email, 19 June 2014; cf. Fergusson, *Life*, p. 20.

3. 'Novelist at Pier Arts Centre', *Orcadian*, 29 March 1990.

4. GMB to Moira Burgess, letter, 6 April 1990.

5. GMB to JR, letter from Aberdeen, 24 April 1990.

6. GMB to JR, letter from Aberdeen, 10 May 1990.

7. GMB to JR, letter from Aberdeen, 24 May 1990.

8. GMB to JR, letter from Aberdeen, 8 June 1990.

9. Fergusson, *Life*, pp. 263–264.

10. Ibid., p. 282.

11. In Brown, *Travellers*, p. 10.

12. Scotia, 1973.

13. Ferguson, *Wound and the Gift*, p. 354.

14. 'Under Brinkie's Brae', *Orcadian*, 4 January 1990; see also 'Impressions of 1989', in Brown, *Rockpools and Daffodils*, p. 229.

15. 'Under Brinkie's Brae', *Orcadian*, 24 October 1991; see also 'Seventy Today', in Brown, *Rockpools and Daffodils*, p. 269.

16. In 'Under Brinkie's Brae: Wheel of the Year', in Brown, *Northern Lights*, p. 47.

17. Ferguson, *Wound and the Gift*, p. 346.

18. Ibid., p. 349.

19. 'Renée Simm: Formidable Proprietor of the Greyfriars Art Shop', *Independent*, 18 November 2005.

20. Ibid.
21. In Joanna Ramsey, *Walking on Hoy* (Glasgow: Galdragon Press, 2002), n.p.
22. A BBC dramatisation of Trollope.
23. *Orcadian*, 24 November 1988; see also 'No Praise for the Dog', in Brown, *Rockpools and Daffodils*, p. 197.
24. Joyce Lindsay and Maurice Lindsay (eds), *The Scottish Dog* (Aberdeen: Aberdeen University Press, 1989).
25. 'Billie Ramsey's Behaviour' (pp. 62–63, emphasis in the original) and 'Consolation in Loneliness' (p. 131), in Brown, *Letters to Gypsy*.
26. See http://www.maxopus.com/life_career.aspx.
27. Sundial Press, 1990.
28. 'Under Brinkie's Brae', *Orcadian*, 11 May 1995; see also George Mackay Brown, 'Drama of a Day's Weather', in *First Wash of Spring*, p. 198.
29. Ferguson, *Wound and the Gift*, p. 346.
30. GMB to JR, letter from Aberdeen, 10 September 1991.
31. GMB to JR, letter from Aberdeen, 14 September 1991.
32. When George copied the acrostic he revised this to 'not / Any Stromnessian can say for sure', but it is reasonably well documented that the Double Houses were built by Christian Robertson.
33. A. M., 'Grand Winter's Night Out', *Orcadian*, 4 February 1992.
34. 'Under Brinkie's Brae', *Orcadian*, 13 August 1992; see also 'A Summer Cold', in Brown, *First Wash of Spring*, p. 50.

4 A BIRTH AND A DEATH

1. From *For the Islands I Sing*, p. 168.
2. GMB to JR, letter from Mayburn Court, 5 June 1993.
3. From 'Mhari', in Brown, *Travellers*, pp. 11–14.
4. GMB to JR, letter from Mayburn Court, 13 June 1993.
5. Brown, *Following a Lark: Poems*, pp. 16–17; see also Brown, *Collected Poems*, pp. 328–329.
6. Fergusson, *Life*, p. 285.
7. 'Stromness New Year's Foy', *Orcadian*, 21 January 1994.
8. *Orcadian*, 10 February 1994; see also 'The Old Black Cat', in Brown, *First Wash of Spring*, p. 134.
9. 'Under Brinkie's Brae', *Orcadian*, 7 July 1994; see also 'Approaching Johnsmas', in Brown, *First Wash of Spring*, p. 155.
10. 'Under Brinkie's Brae', *Orcadian*, 30 June 1994; see also 'A Special Day', in Brown, *First Wash of Spring*, p. 153.

11. Moira Burgess to JR, notes on GMB, May 2014.
12. *Orcadian*, 21 July 1994; see also '80 Victoria Street', in Brown, *First Wash of Spring*, pp. 156–157.
13. Brown, *For the Islands I Sing*, p. 18.
14. GMB to Moira Burgess, letter, 31 July 1994.
15. *Orcadian*, 11 August 1994; see also 'Summer Attractions', in Brown, *First Wash of Spring*, p. 159.
16. John Murray, 1994.
17. Fergusson, *Life*, p. 283.
18. '*Beside the Ocean of Time* by George Mackay Brown: A Booker Prizewinner? Joanna Lawson Spoke to the Author', *Orkney Arts Review*, 5 (1994).
19. 'Under Brinkie's Brae', *Orcadian*, 13 October 1994; see also 'Publicity Operations', in *First Wash of Spring*, p. 168.
20. Ibid., p. 167.
21. 'Edwin Muir and George Mackay Brown: A Study of Two Orkney Poets.'
22. Moira Burgess to JR, notes on GMB, May 2014.
23. 'Under Brinkie's Brae', *Orcadian*, 16 February 1995; see also Brown, 'Seventh Age Has Come Upon Me', in *First Wash of Spring*, p. 189.
24. *Orcadian*, 6 April 1995; see also Brown, ' "New" Writer of Genius', in *First Wash of Spring*, p. 196.
25. *Orcadian*, 25 May 1995; see also 'Sleepless Depression', in Brown, *First Wash of Spring*, p. 200.
26. GMB to Moira Burgess, letter, 8 July 1995.
27. Fergusson, *Life*, p. 287.
28. Ibid.; Ferguson, *Wound and the Gift*, p. 362.
29. In the *Kaleidoscope* programme, 'Interrogating Silence'.
30. Ferguson, *Wound and the Gift*, p. 363.
31. GMB to Moira Burgess, letter, 8 July 1995.
32. A solo piano work which premiered at the St Magnus Festival in 1980.

5 AFTER GEORGE

1. From Morris's preface to Robert Steele, *Medieval Lore from Bartholomew Anglicus*, 1905.
2. *Daily Telegraph*, 15 April 1996. George had one installed at Mayburn Court in 1981: see Fergusson, *Life*, p. 256, footnote.
3. *Herald*, 15 April 1996.
4. *Herald Weekend Extra*, 27 April 1996.

5. *Scotsman*, 15 and 17 April 1996.
6. *Guardian*, 15 April 1996.
7. *Independent*, 15 April 1996.
8. Frank Richardson to JR, letter, 17 April 1996.
9. See Maggie Parham, 'Uncluttered Vision', *Sunday Telegraph Magazine*, 24 September 1995, pp. 18–20.
10. Maggie Parham, 'The Bard of Orkney', *Telegraph Weekend Magazine*, 5 April 1997.
11. See Brown, *For the Islands I Sing*, p. 172.
12. Fergusson, *Life*, p. 244.
13. Paul Harris/Waterfront, 1985; see p. 46.
14. From 'A Work for Poets', in Brown, *Following a Lark*, p. 86.
15. See George Mackay Brown Fellowship website: www.gmbfellowship.org.uk.
16. Colin Baxter Photography, 1996.
17. Black Cygnet Press, 2003.
18. Brown, *Collected Poems*, p. 446.
19. *Northern Times*, 21 September 2007, p. 7.
20. George refers to 'Braal', a variant of the name; see Brown, *For the Islands I Sing*, p. 16.
21. Beth Griffiths to Archie Bevan, letter, 9 June 2008.
22. Beth Griffiths to JR, email, 4 March 2011.
23. See www.georgemackaybrown.co.uk
24. Ferguson, *Wound and the Gift*.
25. *Following a Lark*, p. 34.
26. Loose-leaf pamphlet, Galdragon Press, 1998.
27. *Orcadian*, 10 November 1994; see also 'All Saints' and All Souls' ', in Brown, *First Wash of Spring*, p. 174.
28. Sadly, both Allison Dixon and Archie Bevan died while this book was in production, Allison in December 2014 and Archie in February 2015.
29. Fergusson, *Life*, p. 275.
30. Brown, *Travellers*, p. ix.
31. Ferguson, *Wound and the Gift*, p. 351.
32. From 'Haiku for the Holy Places', in Brown, *Travellers*, p. 38.

SELECT BIBLIOGRAPHY

Allardyce, Keith. *Sea Haven: Stromness in the Orkney Islands*. Photographs by Keith Allardyce and text by Bryce Wilson, with a foreword by George Mackay Brown (Orkney: Orkney Press for Stromness Community Council, 1992).

Bold, Alan. *George Mackay Brown*. Modern Writers series (Edinburgh: Oliver & Boyd, 1978).

Brown, George Mackay. *Andrina and Other Stories* (London: Chatto & Windus/Hogarth Press, 1983).

Brown, George Mackay. *Beside the Ocean of Time* (London: John Murray, 1994).

Brown, George Mackay Brown. *A Calendar of Love and Other Stories* (London: Hogarth Press, 1967).

Brown, George Mackay. *The Collected Poems of George Mackay Brown*. Edited by Archie Bevan and Brian Murray (London: John Murray, 2005).

Brown, George Mackay. *The First Wash of Spring* (London and Edinburgh: Steve Savage, 2006).

Brown, George Mackay. *Fishermen with Ploughs: A Poem Cycle* (London: Hogarth Press, 1971).

Brown, George Mackay. *Following a Lark: Poems* (London: John Murray, 1996).

Brown, George Mackay. *For the Islands I Sing: An Autobiography* (Edinburgh: Polygon, 2008). First published in London by John Murray in 1997.

Brown, George Mackay Brown. *Letters from Hamnavoe* (London and Edinburgh: Steve Savage, 2002). First published by Gordon Wright in 1975.

Brown, George Mackay. *Letters to Gypsy* (Nairn: Balnain Books, 1990).

Brown, George Mackay. *Loaves and Fishes* (London: Hogarth Press, 1959).

Brown, George Mackay. *Magnus: A Novel* (London: Hogarth Press, 1974).

Brown, George Mackay. *The Masked Fisherman and Other Stories* (London: John Murray, 1989).

Brown, George Mackay. *Northern Lights: A Poet's Sources.* Edited by Archie Bevan and Brian Murray (Edinburgh: Polygon, 2007). First published by John Murray in 1999.

Brown, George Mackay. *An Orkney Tapestry.* Drawings by Sylvia Wishart (London: Victor Gollancz, 1969).

Brown, George Mackay Brown. *Portrait of Orkney.* New ed. Photographs by Gunnie Moberg and drawings by Erlend Brown (London: John Murray, 1988). First published in 1981.

Brown, George Mackay. 'The Realms of Gold.' In *Chapman*, special issue on GMB, no. 60 (Spring 1990), pp. 24–31.

Brown, George Mackay. *Rockpools and Daffodils: An Orcadian Diary 1979–1991* (Edinburgh: Gordon Wright, 1992).

Brown, George Mackay. *Three Plays: The Loom of Light, The Well and The Voyage of Saint Brandon* (London: Chatto & Windus/Hogarth Press, 1984).

Brown, George Mackay. *Time in a Red Coat* (Harmondsworth: Penguin Books, 1986). First published by Chatto & Windus/Hogarth Press, 1984.

Brown, George Mackay. *A Time to Keep and Other Stories* (London: Hogarth Press, 1976).

Brown, George Mackay. *Travellers: Poems*. Edited with an introduction by Archie Bevan and Brian Murray (London: John Murray, 2001).

Brown, George Mackay. *The Wreck of the Archangel: Poems* (London: John Murray, 1989).

Catlin, Angela. *Natural Light: Portraits of Scottish Writers* (Edinburgh: Paul Harris/Waterfront, 1985).

Ferguson, Ron. *George Mackay Brown: The Wound and the Gift* (Edinburgh: St Andrew's Press, 2011).

Fergusson, Maggie. *George Mackay Brown: The Life* (London: John Murray, 2006; paperback edition, 2007).

Moberg, Gunnie, and George Mackay Brown. *Orkney: Pictures and Poems* (Grantown-on-Spey: Colin Baxter Photography, 1996).

Murray, Rowena, and Brian Murray. *Interrogation of Silence: The Writings of George Mackay Brown* (London: John Murray, 2004).

Ramsey, Joanna. *In Memory of George Mackay Brown* (Glasgow: Galdragon Press, 1998).

Ramsey, Joanna. *Walking on Hoy* (Glasgow: Galdragon Press, 2002).

Rendall, Robert. *Collected Poems*. Edited and introduction by John Flett Brown and Brian Murray (London and Edinburgh: Steve Savage, 2012).

Shoal and Sheaf: Orkney's Pictorial Heritage. Selection and commentary by David M. N. Tinch, photographic reproduction by David Mackie, and an introduction by George Mackay Brown (Kirkwall: Orkney Library, 1988).

Sylvia Wishart: A Study. With an essay by Mel Gooding, an introduction by Neil Firth, and personal recollections by Ola Gorie and Elsie Seatter (Stromness: Pier Arts Centre, 2012).

INDEX